*Hope's Reprise*

# Hope's Reprise

*David Newman*

TRANSLATED FROM YIDDISH BY MIRIAM BECKERMAN

THE AZRIELI FOUNDATION
www.azrielifoundation.org

Cover and book design by Mark Goldstein
Endpaper maps by Martin Gilbert
Map on page xxxv by François Blanc
Cover image of "The Buchenwald March" courtesy of Ronald Leopoldi

LIBRARY AND ARCHIVES CANADA CATALOGUING IN PUBLICATION

Newman, David, 1919–2002, author
       Hope's reprise / David Newman; Miriam Beckerman, translator.

(The Azrieli series of holocaust survivor memoirs; 7)
Includes index.
ISBN 978-1-897470-89-3 (paperback)

1. Newman, David, 1919–2002. 2. Holocaust, Jewish (1939–1945) – Poland – Personal narratives. 3. Jews – Poland – Biography. 4. Holocaust survivors – Canada – Biography. I. Beckerman, Miriam Dashkin, translator II. Azrieli Foundation, issuing body III. Title.

DS134.72.N48A313 2015      940.53'18092      C2015-905912-7

PRINTED IN CANADA

# The Azrieli Series of Holocaust Survivor Memoirs

Naomi Azrieli, Publisher

Jody Spiegel, Program Director
Arielle Berger, Managing Editor
Elizabeth Lasserre, Senior Editor, French-Language Editions
Farla Klaiman, Editor
Elin Beaumont, Senior Educational Outreach and Events Coordinator
Catherine Person, Educational Outreach and Events Coordinator,
    Quebec and French Canada
Marc-Olivier Cloutier, Educational Outreach and Events Assistant,
    Quebec and French Canada
Tim MacKay, Digital Platform Manager
Elizabeth Banks, Digital Asset and Archive Curator
Susan Roitman, Office Manager (Toronto)
Mary Mellas, Executive Assistant and Human Resources (Montreal)

Mark Goldstein, Art Director
François Blanc, Cartographer
Bruno Paradis, Layout, French-language editions

# Contents

# Series Preface:
# In their own words. . .

*In telling these stories, the writers have liberated themselves. For so many years we did not speak about it, even when we became free people living in a free society. Now, when at last we are writing about what happened to us in this dark period of history, knowing that our stories will be read and live on, it is possible for us to feel truly free. These unique historical documents put a face on what was lost, and allow readers to grasp the enormity of what happened to six million Jews – one story at a time.*

*David J. Azrieli*, C.M., C.Q., M.Arch
Holocaust survivor and founder, The Azrieli Foundation

Since the end of World War II, over 30,000 Jewish Holocaust survivors have immigrated to Canada. Who they are, where they came from, what they experienced and how they built new lives for themselves and their families are important parts of our Canadian heritage. The Azrieli Foundation's Holocaust Survivor Memoirs Program was established to preserve and share the memoirs written by those who survived the twentieth-century Nazi genocide of the Jews of Europe and later made their way to Canada. The program is guided by the conviction that each survivor of the Holocaust has a remarkable story to tell, and that such stories play an important role in education about tolerance and diversity.

Millions of individual stories are lost to us forever. By preserving the stories written by survivors and making them widely available to a broad audience, the Azrieli Foundation's Holocaust Survivor Memoirs Program seeks to sustain the memory of all those who perished at the hands of hatred, abetted by indifference and apathy. The personal accounts of those who survived against all odds are as different as the people who wrote them, but all demonstrate the courage, strength, wit and luck that it took to prevail and survive in such terrible adversity. The memoirs are also moving tributes to people – strangers and friends – who risked their lives to help others, and who, through acts of kindness and decency in the darkest of moments, frequently helped the persecuted maintain faith in humanity and courage to endure. These accounts offer inspiration to all, as does the survivors' desire to share their experiences so that new generations can learn from them.

The Holocaust Survivor Memoirs Program collects, archives and publishes these distinctive records and the print editions are available free of charge to educational institutions and Holocaust-education programs across Canada. They are also available for sale to the general public at bookstores. All revenues to the Azrieli Foundation from the sales of the Azrieli Series of Holocaust Survivor Memoirs go toward the publishing and educational work of the memoirs program.

⁓

The Azrieli Foundation would like to express appreciation to the following people for their invaluable efforts in producing this book: Miriam Beckerman, Doris Bergen, Sherry Dodson (Maracle Press), Barbara Kamieński, Ronald Leopoldi, Malcolm Lester, Therese Parent, Bret Werb, and Margie Wolfe and Emma Rodgers of Second Story Press.

# About the Glossary

The following memoir contains a number of terms, concepts and historical references that may be unfamiliar to the reader. For information on major organizations; significant historical events and people; geographical locations; religious and cultural terms; and foreign-language words and expressions that will help give context and background to the events described in the text, please see the glossary beginning on page 103.

# Introduction

David Newman was a beloved member of the Toronto Jewish community, where he was known as "Mr. Borochov" for co-founding the
Kol Yisroel congregation at the Borochov Centre, the home of Labour
Zionism in the city. In the 1950s, he appeared prominently in Yiddish
vaudeville and, for many years thereafter, he taught Yiddish classes,
performed in Yiddish theatre, chaired the Yiddish Cultural Council
and did Yiddish translation for the city courts. Newman headed the
Labour Zionist Alliance in Toronto, was active in the Workmen's
Circle and was a well-known activist, raising funds for Israel. In the
1980s, as he began to share his Holocaust experiences before audienc-
es in schools and synagogues, Newman wrote a memoir in Yiddish.
His son, Jack, located the memoir when David Newman died in
2002.[1] The death of "the Yiddishist David Newman" in Canada was
noted at the time as a great loss by the *American Jewish Year Book*.[2]
This current English account – superbly translated by prize-winning
translator Miriam Dashkin Beckerman – is an edited version of the
earlier manuscript, written at the beginning of the remarkable up-
surge of memoir writing by Holocaust survivors in North America
during the 1980s.

---

1  "Mr. Borochov Dies at 82," *Canadian Jewish News* (January 17, 2002).
2  *American Jewish Year Book* (New York: American Jewish Committee, 2003), p. 333.

Each Holocaust memoir is important, for each tells a specific story, memorializing lost people and places that ceased to exist under Nazi power. Each is also important in making the large story of the Holocaust accessible to readers at the micro-level, permitting them to see in granular detail the kinds of experiences and dilemmas that marked everyday life and death for Jews under the pressures of Nazi rule. David Newman's memoir is valuable in both these ways, drawing our attention to his story – and his family's story – in the small town ghettos of southwest Poland and in several Nazi labour and concentration camps. But David Newman's memoir is also significant in providing a specific window into the Holocaust as it unfolded in western Poland during the early 1940s through the formation of ghettos and the Nazi deportations to Treblinka. He draws our attention to the demanding slave labour experiences of the small remnant of Jews who, alongside and after the deportations, were selected for work and endured under horrific conditions. Finally, he casts light on a little known episode involving the rescue of children and youths inside a Nazi concentration camp, Buchenwald, in which he was recruited to play a small but important role.

～

David Newman (David Eliezer Najman) was born in Chmielnik in the Kielce district of Poland on December 11, 1919, the son of Yitzhak and Chanah Najman, both of whom were natives of the small industrial and trading town. Chmielnik was located about thirty-two kilometres southeast of Kielce and 112 kilometres northeast of Krakow in western Galicia. The area had been in the Habsburg Empire before World War I and was then incorporated into reborn Poland. Chmielnik's Jewish population grew during the Second Polish Republic, nearly doubling between 1921 and 1939. David's father was a modern man and a committed member of the Poalei Zion; he was also a well-known leader in Yiddish theatre in the town and throughout the region. The family was part of a network of families linked by kinship in the city and in several towns nearby.

In 1938, after the death of his mother, David, his three sisters and his father moved from Chmielnik to Lodz, the second largest city in Poland, where one-third of the inhabitants were Jews. Father and son found employment teaching at the I. Pasternak School and the family was in the early stages of adjusting to big city life when that life was disrupted by the Nazi invasion. David Newman did not write much in *Hope's Reprise* about what was taking place in Lodz at this time, when Jewish businesses were being "Aryanized," Jews were being barred from public transport and, in November, ordered to wear yellow badges. Amid the deepening persecution preceding creation of the ghetto, which occurred in February 1940, the Najman family reasoned they might be better off moving back to Chmielnik, where many relatives resided. Unable to locate permanent living arrangements in Chmielnik, the family left again, this time to relatives in nearby Staszów, thirty-two kilometres further to the east.

Newman's memoir offers us particular insight into this active agency exercised by many Polish Jewish families early on during the Nazi occupation – travelling back to their towns of origin to reunite with members of their extended families and improve their situations. Ghetto creation evolved slowly under the Nazis in the larger cities during 1939-1941, but more slowly in the smaller *shtetlach* (rural market towns) of western Poland. It was possible, initially, to strategize where conditions might be best and resources might be most available. While a ghetto was created in Chmielnik in April 1941, there was no ghetto in Staszów until June 1942. Beyond relocating, Polish Jewish agency extended to forms of active maneuvering in order to sustain life inside the Nazi ghettos. *Hope's Reprise* illustrates how, even as the death camps were fully operating but yet unknown in the ghettos, David and his family – and others – sought to assist each other through mutual self-help initiatives to increase chances for survival. These Polish Jews made no passive reconciliation with their fate, but actively sought to take advantage of openings in the Nazi web of terror to endure and survive.

After the Staszów ghetto was formed, and amid growing rumours of ghetto liquidations and deportations eastward during the summer and fall of 1942 (roughly the time the Warsaw ghetto was being emptied), desperate families and individuals – David and his family among them – strategically sought to get work in a tailor shop, making garments for the German army, to avoid being transported to an unknown destination. In connection with this effort, David learned from his cousin Efraim Zyngier, who headed the Jewish community in Staszów, that a few hundred young people from Staszów were being supplied to work in a munitions operation in nearby Skarżysko-Kamienna. Under pressure to increase the labour contingent, Efraim Zyngier promised David that his father and sisters would get places in the tailor shop if he would volunteer for Skarżysko.[3] So David reported to the Staszówer Judenrat, he writes, in September 1942, and was sent north to Skarżysko shortly after. On November 8, the Nazis deported 8,000 Jews from Staszów to Treblinka, sparing David's family as essential workers in the war industry.[4]

Even so, David's father and sisters were eventually deported to the Poniatowa labour camp and murdered there by the Nazis during an operation known well to historians as the *Aktion Erntefest* (Operation Harvest Festival) in November 1943. That year, after uprisings in Warsaw and Bialystok and in the death camps of Treblinka and Sobibor, the Nazis killed all remaining prisoners in the labour camps in the Lublin district, including Poniatowa, Trawniki and Majdanek. The Nazis did not destroy Skarżysko-Kamienna, in the Radom district, where David Newman worked making ammunition until mid-1944.

Skarżysko-Kamienna, located seventy-seven kilometres to the

---

3  Efraim Zyngier, David Newman's cousin, was president of the Staszów community and perished during the deportations, according to the Shoah Names Database at Yad Vashem in Israel. See Bilski testimony, Item 681114.

4  The date David Newman went to Skarżysko was likely October 8, and the day of the community's destruction was November 8, 1942, the 28th day of Heshvan, 5703, in the Jewish calendar. The Jews from Staszów were taken to Treblinka and also to Belzec.

north from Staszów, a bit above Kielce, housed a sprawling manufacturing operation comprised of three separate factory camps surrounded by barbed wire and guard towers and guarded by SS soldiers
and Ukrainian police. Werk A was the largest section and, with Werk
B, produced ammunition for the *Wehrmacht*; in Werk C, prisoners
fashioned explosives and chemicals into grenades, bombs and underwater mines. The Skarżysko camp was infamous because the slave
labourers in Werk C worked with the dangerous yellow chemicals,
Trotyl (TNT) and picric acid, normally without protective gloves or
glasses. Their eyes and skin quickly turned yellow, causing them to
appear as macabre yellow figures; many also suffered extreme kid-
ney failure, and died. Seeing prisoners in Werk C upon first arriving at Skarżysko, many former prisoners testify, struck terror into
their hearts, reinforcing their sense that entering the camp was entering "another planet." Conditions for workers elsewhere in the camp
were horrific in other ways: the operation was rife with disease and
epidemics; the food was insufficient; camp guards and functionaries treated prisoners brutally; and any prisoners unable to work were
vulnerable to being removed and shot in the nearby forest.

In a first-rate history titled *Death Comes in Yellow*, Felicja Karay,
a survivor of the camp who became a fine historian, offers a broad
picture of the recruitment process that brought thousands of Jewish prisoners from small towns in the Radom District – Chmielnik,
Opatów, Ożarów, Staszów, Stopnica, Suchedniów and Zwoleń – to the
camp in October-November 1942,[5] which she labels the Radom era.
The numbers of prisoners were augmented the next year by additional groups of Jewish prisoners brought from Majdanek and from
Płaszów during June and November 1943 respectively.

David Newman takes us inside Skarżysko-Kamienna and describes well the largest ammunition operation in the Nazi Gener-

---

5  See Felicja Karay, *Death Comes in Yellow: Skarżysko-Kamienna Slave Labor Camp*
   (Amsterdam: Harwood Academic Publishers, 1996), p. 36.

al-government, run by the powerful HASAG corporation [Hugo Schneider Aktiengesellschaft]. David Newman slaved in this camp for twenty-one months until he and other prisoners were sent to Buchenwald as the Soviet Army advanced nearby. Newman writes of the complicated social relations in a camp in which Jewish prisoner functionaries kept order and served Nazi needs while presiding over a corrupted moral order. Internally the camp was administered under the command of Frau Fela Markowiczowa, whose family controlled the Jewish police and distribution of provisions. This strata of camp functionaries could ease or make more harsh individual life chances for prisoners. Karay describes how the strata – comprised of *prominente*, prominent families tied to the camp leaders and also the Jewish police; *courtiers*, lower-level prisoner functionaries, hangers-on of the leadership; and money barons who controlled the camp black market – had arrogated to themselves special privileges in the camp.[6]

Newman also illuminates what may be very surprising to readers – the existence in the camp of a narrow social space for prisoner-initiated cultural activities, including the writing of poems and stories and the performances of weekly concerts, poetry readings, story readings and sketches about Lager life in an effort to make imprisonment and slavery palatable. Markowiczowa and her functionaries served as the unlikely patrons of cultural production in Skarżysko. Karay writes that Markowiczowa, the royal queen in a harsh and cruel world, viewed it as a privilege of her power to patronize the arts and to protect artists and performers. Camp performances, or concerts, began during fall 1943 when camp conditions loosened a bit. Programs consisted of songs in Yiddish and Polish, poetry readings, skits and satires depicting camp life. Bund members from Warsaw who came via Majdanek added songs of the Jewish proletariat and accounted for the heavy dose of *Yiddishkeit* in the concerts. A res-

---

6   Ibid., p. 99.

cue committee established by Bund and Poalei Zion members also collected bread fees at the concerts, redistributing provisions to the needy.[7]

Mordechai Strigler, a Yiddish writer originally from Zamość and then Warsaw, an exceptional talent who would later edit *Der Yiddishe Kemfer*, a Yiddish literary magazine, and serve as the last editor of the Yiddish *Forward*, wrote original Yiddish poems and performed them at Skarżysko. Newman also wrote and sang songs, performing alone and with other singers. When Newman met Mordechai Strigler, he noted that Strigler made the Sunday concerts richer in content. It was Newman, however, who wrote the song "In the Skarżysko Lager," which ended each camp concert with performers and prisoners standing and singing the song together "like a hymn." Numerous other talented prisoners played a variety of roles, including the poets Ilona and Henryka Karmel and the violinist and musicologist Mosze Imber. By spring 1944, the concerts were put on regularly for the whole camp. Camp commandants and German managers attended the events, taking up the first row benches; prisoners sat or stood around the edges. Karay says these concerts helped keep order in the camp and, at the same time, were forms of resistance, encouraging feelings of hope and solidarity while affirming human endurance and creativity amidst ongoing degradation.[8] Newman confirms they "were a balm for the physically and spiritually broken prisoners."

---

7  Christopher Browning writes that "an extraordinary cultural life, especially expressed in song, flourished." Like Karay, Browning understands Markowiczowa's support as due to her desire to be entertained and also to advance her own self-image as a court patron. Review of *Death Comes in Yellow*, by Felicja Karay, in *Holocaust and Genocide Studies* 12:3 (1998), p. 477.

8  Felicja Karay, "Teaching the Holocaust Through Music and Camp Literature Written in the Camps," paper presented at Yad Vashem International Education Conference, October 13, 1999, available at http://www.yadvashem.org/download/education/conf/Karay.pdf

When David Newman fell ill with typhus and was moved to the quarantine barrack, Markowiczowa sent the performer warm tea; when SS soldiers came to take prisoners from the barrack to be murdered, Markowiczowa sent a functionary to save him. David Newman, it is clear, had become a favoured prisoner performer, sponsored by the Jewish leadership in Skarżysko, and was a key figure in cultural production in the camp. Eventually, Markowiczowa got Newman a job with her Jewish police, sharply increasing his chances for survival and giving him more time for his cultural activities. In his new role, Newman met Hanka, who had come from Płaszów and who later, after the war, would become his wife. When the camp was evacuated at the end of July 1944, Newman was then brought with other male prisoners on a large transport to Buchenwald.

When the locked doors of the cattle cars opened at the concentration camp near Weimar on August 5, the prisoners were organized for registration and given uniforms and numbers; Newman became prisoner number 68577. The prisoners were met by several veteran Polish Jewish prisoners, including camp brick-masons Gustav Schiller from Lwów and Elek Grinbaum from Tarnów. Schiller and Grinbaum addressed the newcomers in Yiddish and reassured them not to be afraid: there were no gas chambers here and the underground had significant influence in the camp. The primary job of the emissaries sent to meet the transport was to learn who in Skarżysko had brutalized prisoners and collaborated with the Nazis. Their first goal was to protect the underground against potential threats coming into the camp. David Newman reports that six persons from the train, including some Jewish policemen, were given crude justice in the next few days. An additional job for these men was to identify and find children and youths.

Newman's memoir is enlightening in its description of Buchenwald and the remarkable, clandestine child- and youth-saving operation that evolved there. At Buchenwald, the German Communist-led international resistance ran the internal self-administration in uneasy collaboration with the Nazi SS.[9] The German Communists were wrong ideologically to the Nazi leaders but were right racially, ethnically and linguistically: they were an organized, disciplined force that was capable of serving as a middle management, helping keep order and running the camp efficiently. This was important to the Nazis as Buchenwald transformed in scale and size after 1942, becoming a large transit camp receiving and distributing thousands of prisoners to satellite camps important to the war economy. Collaboration with the Nazis in overseeing parts of the camp, paradoxically, gave opportunities to the Communist-led international resistance to use its favoured positions in the administrative institutions, warehouses, barracks and work commandos of the camp for clandestine resistance. Such resistance initially included saving selected prisoners with the right political views and, late in 1943, expanded to protecting children. *Hope's Reprise* offers readers a brief, revealing glimpse into this child and youth rescue initiative, in which David Newman participated from August to December 1944.

Most of the prisoners arriving from Skarżysko were placed in quarantine in the Kleines Lager (little camp) for a time, and then were sent to Schlieben, another HASAG factory camp located further east where prisoners were making *Panzerfaust*, hand-held German anti-tank weapons. David Newman and Mordechai Strigler, with a few other prisoners, were spared transport to the satellite camp and were instead picked out and placed in a barrack in the Grosse Lager (main camp), a new Jewish block, where conditions were better. This was block 23, which was filled, as he accurately recalls, with "Jewish veterans from various European countries," many of whom belonged to "active anti-Nazi movements."

---

9  Eugen Kogan, *The Theory and Practice of Hell: The German Concentration Camps and the System Behind Them* (New York: Farrar Straus and Giroux, 1950, 2006), pp. 251 ff., esp 256-257, 267-268. See also the Buchenwald prisoner Christopher Burney's memoir, *Dungeon Democracy* (New York: Duell, Sloan, and Pierce, 1946).

A small number of veteran Jewish prisoners in Buchenwald linked with the German Communist-led international underground had been appointed as staff in the new Jewish block, 23, in summer 1944. This group of men, acting with the approval of the Communist-led resistance but also in accordance with their own dynamic and outlook, recruited prisoners off the new transports to assist them in working with Jewish youths who were then arriving from labour camps in western Poland. These newcomers, like David Newman and Mordechai Strigler, were selected to work with and oversee and teach children whom the veteran Jewish prisoners were gathering under their mentorship and direction. Their role was to keep the minds of the children occupied and to help lift their spirits. David Newman tells how he and Strigler led the youths in story and in song in the barrack. The children and youths were clustered in children's blocks, protected against transport to Buchenwald's outer camps where work was killing, kept from work or assigned to benign tasks, and provided occasional access to extra food. In addition, they were provided with rudimentary schooling.

Newman was also assigned to work in a construction commando near the Gustloff Armament Werke just outside the gate at Buchenwald, where he witnessed the pinpoint Allied bombing on August 24, 1944, of the Nazi factory. The Germans were making rifles and parts at the Gustloff plant for the V1 and V2 rockets that were then being fashioned at nearby Dora, another Buchenwald satellite. The rest of his time, working with Mordechai Strigler, was devoted to mentoring and teaching Jewish children in the barrack. One child from the transport, Martin (Menek) Schiller, from Tarnobrzeg, whose brother was in block 23, went there frequently, and observes in a recent testimony at the Yiddish Book Center in Massachusetts that a school functioned there. The school, he says, was led by the writer Mordechai Strigler, who wrote Yiddish songs and little vignettes, as well as by other prisoners, and the youths in the school sang songs in Yiddish. One song was about how youths who had witnessed death and suffered terrible losses could nonetheless laugh and still be hopeful. Another was about revolution, youths in the future who would be "coming marching on" carrying a red flag.[10]

Jack (Yakov) Werber, another veteran Jewish prisoner in Buchenwald originally from Radom, was the *Schreiber* (secretary) in block 23 under a Communist block elder, Karl Siegmeyer, and was also part of the Jewish group linked with the underground committed to saving children. In his powerful memoir, *Saving Children,* Werber describes the schooling effort in the barrack, mentioning David Newman, who "had a beautiful voice" and "gave the children singing instruction."[11] Werber also discusses Mordechai Strigler, who "gave the children hope by telling them stories of Jewish resistance and courage in the past and promising that one day they would have revenge against their tormentors." It was not easy, Werber assesses: many children were traumatized by their experiences, deprived of their families who had been killed, and were "cynical" and "old beyond their years." David Newman, Mordechai Strigler and others tried to give them hope that a tomorrow existed and to convince them they would survive to return to normal life when the war ended. When Buchenwald was liberated in April 1945, after Newman was gone, nearly 1,000 children and youths remained alive, including several score who had been brought from Skarżysko.

Mordechai Strigler remained in Buchenwald working with children until liberation but David Newman was sent out on December 13, 1944, to Berga-Elster. There, prisoners worked breaking stones

---

10 Interview with Martin Schiller by Mark Gerstein, June 13, 2013, at http://www. yiddishbookcenter.org/oral-history/martin-schiller, Wexler Oral History Project, Yiddish Book Center, Amherst, MA. See also Martin Schiller, *Bread, Butter, and Sugar: A Boy's Journey Through the Holocaust and Postwar Europe* (Lanham, MD: Hamilton Books, 2007), pp. 46-47.

11 Jack Werber, *Saving Children: Diary of a Buchenwald Survivor and Rescuer* (New Brunswick, NJ: Transaction Publishers, 1996), p. 101.

and rocks and digging underground tunnels for a planned armaments factory. In *Hope's Reprise*, Newman writes it was difficult to say farewell to the Jewish children he taught, but the resistance in Buchenwald had put a list together and anticipated some influence over events and conditions at Berga. Nonetheless, work at Berga turned out to be difficult and extremely taxing during the winter of 1945 and, in addition to the harsh work and extreme cold, all the prisoners grew increasingly anxious in the last months as the Allied armies came from both west and east. It was unclear if the Germans would kill all the prisoners before they could be liberated. David Newman's difficult time at Berga was then topped off by a Nazi-led death march beginning April 10, 1945, as the Soviets approached, on which surviving prisoners were ultimately brought to the Czech-German border and to a Czech town near Pilsen. Somehow, with a strong mind still committed to resisting, Newman made contact with Czech partisans in the town, and he and some friends walked away from the march with help from Czech protectors. David Newman and his friends found shelter among the Czechs until the war's end on May 8.

After David Newman's experiences in several camps and on the death march, the young man, now twenty-six, faced the challenging task, like other survivors emerging from the camps, of determining – what now? Who will I be and where will I be? With what seems remarkable stamina and determination after all that he had experienced, David Newman returned to Lodz and to Warsaw, seeking other survivors, particularly family members. Within months, he got productive work in Lodz, where many Polish Jewish survivors were gathering, and he found and brought Hanka (Anna) to Lodz from her town of Tarnów. The couple was married in Lodz during fall 1945. At that point, assessing clearly the difficult realities Jewish survivors faced in post-war Poland, David and Hanka left with false papers, travelling illegally to Germany by train and arriving eventually at the Landsberg Displaced Persons camp in the American zone.

David Newman worked in provisions in the hospital and soon again became actively involved in cultural work. A choir and theatre group began, concerts took place weekly and theatre performances were booked for other DP camps and in nearby Munich. Interestingly, the theatre performances now were a little less about spiritual resistance and a little more informed by survivors' wartime experiences and their need to memorialize lost family and friends. At Landsberg, for example, some of the plays included the following: *Kiddush Hashem* (the phrase meaning Jewish martyrdom), *Yizkor* (the Jewish prayer for the dead) and *Ich Leb* (I Live).[12] There were also performances reclaiming classic Yiddish theatre pieces remembered from before the war.

While they were living in the camp in Landsberg, somehow an uncle of David's living in Paris found and made contact with David, and, after their first child, Yitzhak (Isaac) was born, the new family left for the French capital. Living in the city rather than yet another camp and making one's own living was more attractive to David and his new bride than staying in Landsberg. In Paris, they lived in the Marais near Rue des Rosiers and David worked with his uncle, learning tailoring, and began adjusting to a new life. However, this was not to be the family's final destination. After five challenging years in France, in April 1951 David and his family immigrated to Canada.

There, as his son observes in an afterword, David constructed life anew with the same commitment and hopefulness he had exhibited in the camps, in the process bestowing gifts on all who came to

---

12 Michael Brenner, *After the Holocaust: Rebuilding Jewish Lives in Postwar Germany* (Princeton: Princeton University Press, 1999), p. 28. See also Margery Myers Feinstein, "Reimagining the Unimaginable: Theatre, Memory, and Rehabilitation in the Displaced Persons Camps," in *After the Holocaust: Challenging the Myth of Silence*, eds., David Cesarani and Eric Sundquist (New York: Routledge, 2012), pp. 39 ff.

know him – gifts of laughter, music, literature, love of theatre and Yiddish, and of poetry. He remained thoughtfully engaged with Jewish life, culture and religion in Toronto, and he actively promoted useful causes, especially support for Israel. He earned a living initially as a tailor and later as a small businessman. But David Newman remained most comfortable in the classroom, on the stage, at the microphone at events, and later as a guest speaker bearing witness about the Holocaust in schools. At his funeral in 2002, a fellow member of the Yiddish Cultural Council, Simcha Simchovitch, said simply, "He was loved by a lot of people." Despite what he had endured and lost, despite even the hardships that demanded starting over several times, he embraced life fully and had a positive outlook. He had occasional "sad moments," like many survivors, his son says, but these were passing moments for someone who loved, enjoyed and took pride in his family and his community work, and who, in later years, enjoyed travelling with Anna, returning to France and visiting Israel.

When Roberto Benigni's film *Life is Beautiful* appeared in the late 1990s, a fabulistic representation of a father and a young child in a Nazi concentration camp, David's son, Jack, asked his father whether there could have been children in the Nazi camps. "Oh yes," David responded, "there were children, yes, sure, there were children in the camp at Buchenwald, and we were teaching them."[13] What could better represent a positive outlook than teaching children to hope inside a Nazi concentration camp?

*Kenneth Waltzer*
Michigan State University
2015

---

13 Phone Interview with Jack Newman by the author, July 8, 2015.

# Acknowledgements

For cover image of "The Buchenwald March" by Hermann Leopoldi and Dr. Löhna-Beda

Hermann Leopoldi (1888–1959) described himself as a "piano humorist." His songs, witty and satirical, mirrored the political and social upheavals of his time and enthralled his audience. Leopoldi's work evolved in an astonishing range of environments – from the Vienna coffee houses of the 1920s and '30s through the concentration camp at Buchenwald to the club scene in Manhattan during his exile.

In March 1938, after the annexation of Austria to the German Third Reich, the Nazis increased the persecution of Jews and other races. From one day to another, celebrity, esteem and merit no longer existed and, as a Jew, Hermann Leopoldi was targeted by the National Socialist regime. Hermann Leopoldi tried to flee from Austria to Czechoslovakia and obtain an exit visa, but the new regime barred him from leaving. Shortly after, he was taken to an inquiry at the police station, from where he never came back. Leopoldi had been deported to Dachau. On September 22, 1938, he was transported to Buchenwald.

The following is an excerpt from Leopoldi's memoirs, *The Life of a Viennese Piano Humorist*, describing how the "Buchenwald March" came to be:

*There was no norm or reference point for the way one should conduct oneself because in Buchenwald it was boundless caprice alone that ruled.*

*Commandant Koch, who ran the camp, rarely made an appearance, delegating his authority to his deputy Rödl, a Bavarian with an unparalleled lack of intelligence. One of his favorite pastimes was to have the camp prisoners sing folk tunes and children's lullabies for his personal pleasure. After a while, our children's songs must have gotten on his nerves because one day he roared – roaring being his natural mode of expression – "Write something about Buchenwald! A march! Ten marks for the best one! Something fine! Go on, get to it! Dismissed!"*

*We couldn't believe our ears. Once over our astonishment, we engaged in a camp-wide competition that was without parallel. Among other things, I wrote, together with Dr. Beda, the Buchenwald March, which the commandant liked best and which he accepted. No doubt that won us the competition, but we never did get the promised prize of ten marks.*

*This march now became his favourite song, so that we had to sing it at all times and on all occasions. Naturally, my comrades and I sang the song with tremendous enthusiasm, feeling the revolutionary spirit within it.*

*It is the surest sign of the commandant's low intelligence that he himself noticed nothing of the unbelievably revolutionary spirit of this song and could wax so enthusiastic over it. That he was extremely fond of the song is clear, because he said to his underlings, "I can't tell them this, but that is one helluva march!" "Helluva" was the highest praise he could bestow with his very modest vocabulary.*

*The song was rehearsed in all the blocks and the prison band had to play it eighty to a hundred times a day. Even the block I was in rehearsed it. We stood in rows before the SS. The last word of the song, "frei" (free), was supposed to be sung quite tersely and clipped, in German military style.*

*At the first command performance of the song I sang along myself and held the last note as long as the melody actually required. But since the others, without exception, had cut off the last syllable very abruptly, my voice continued ringing out as a solo. So this livid SS-man descends on me shouting, "You idiot! Can't you sing? Who are you?"*

*In strict military posture I inform him, "I am the composer of this song!" Whereupon followed something unimaginable – an explosion of laughter in this horrible setting!*

Leopoldi's friend and lyricist of the "Buchenwald March," Dr. Löhna-Beda, died in Auschwitz in 1942. Hermann Leopoldi left Buchenwald on February 21, 1939. On March 20, 1939, he arrived in New York, and in his first gesture as a free man, he fell down to his knees and kissed American soil, the soil of the country that had restored his faith in humanity and in freedom.

## THE BUCHENWALD MARCH

*By grey dawn we prisoners head out*
*For another day of hard labour,*
*A crust of bread in our sacks*
*And care in our hearts.*

*How I miss my girl,*
*So far away. Is she faithful?*
*We carry shovel and pickaxe,*
*And love in our hearts.*

*Short nights, long days.*
*Courage, comrades, stay the course,*
*For our blood pulses with the will to live*
*And our hearts with faith.*

Refrain:

*Oh Buchenwald, unforgettable, you are my fate.*
*To leave you is to know freedom.*
*But we'll not wail or whine;*
*We'll answer yes to life,*
*Come what may,*
*For one day we'll be free.*

Map

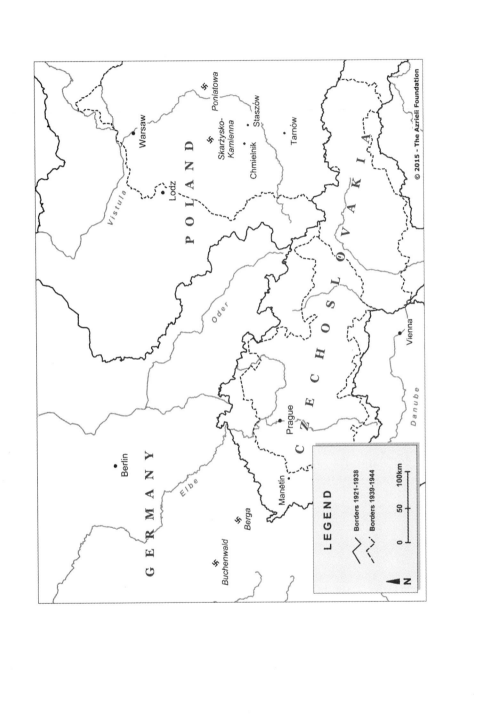

**LEGEND**

Borders 1921-1938
Borders 1939-1944

0    50    100km

N

GERMANY

Berlin

Buchenwald

Berga

Elbe

Manětín

Prague

CZECHOSLOVAKIA

Vienna

Danube

POLAND

Vistula

Warsaw

Lodz

Oder

Skarżysko-
Kamienna

Poniatowa

Chmielnik

Staszów

Tarnów

© 2015 - The Azrieli Foundation

In memory of my father, Itchele Neiman, and my three sisters, Tova Leah, Faigele and Rokhelle, who perished in World War II together with six million Kedoshim.

# My Hometown

My father, Yitzhak, or Itchele as he was called, was a teacher in the town of Chmielnik, Poland. In 1919, the year I was born, he was hired to teach Yiddish and music in many of the Jewish organizations, which had newly established drama groups. My father was their first drama teacher and the theatre director for various other groups as well. He organized theatre productions in both Hebrew and Yiddish with the children of the girls' school, Yavne. It was very festive in town whenever there was a theatrical presentation – *Shulamith*, for example – or a play about a historical subject, such as Bar Kokhba or Uriel Acosta.[1] Theatrical groups from Warsaw, Lodz and other cities in Poland toured the smaller towns, and Chmielnik became a destination for Jewish theatre lovers. All the performances were crowned with success.

Chmielnik is situated in the eastern part of Poland between the city of Kielce and the resort town of Busko-Zdrój. Gravestones in the cemetery dated back eight hundred years, showing that Jews had been in the area since the 1200s, but most recorded information states that Sephardic Jews expelled from Spain started moving into Chmielnik in the seventeenth century. The Jewish population, though small in

---

1  For information on *Shulamith*, Bar Kokhba and Uriel Acosta, as well as on other historical, religious and cultural terms; significant historical events and people; geographical locations; major organizations; and foreign-language words and expressions contained in the text, please see the glossary.

number, erected a beautiful synagogue that was completed in 1638. The Jewish community's main work was in raising cattle, and when trade began to develop on a small scale, some Jews began trading in wood and textiles.

In the mid-seventeenth century, the Chmielnicki Uprising and the Swedish invasion of Poland caused a bloodbath in many Jewish towns, including Chmielnik. In 1655, the army of Stefan Czarniecki carried out an organized mass killing, taking revenge on the Jewish population for supposedly assisting the Swedish army during the invasion. One hundred and fifty Jews were slaughtered in Chmielnik.

By 1764, there were some 1,400 Jews living in Chmielnik. Gradually, the non-Jewish population began to tolerate their Jewish neighbours and, with the town united, Chmielnik grew both economically and in number of residents.

At the end of the eighteenth century, the first group of Hasidim was established under the leadership of Reb Avraham David Orbach, who was also the leader of the recently established Jewish *kehilla*, a communal, religious governing group. I've heard that the first group of Hasidim ever to make aliyah to Jaffa, in what was then called Palestine, came from Chmielnik. The Hasidim founded Chmielnik's first yeshiva, and their strong influence continued through the nineteenth century.

Jews came to Chmielnik from various parts of the country to take advantage of the opportunities afforded by the stable economy – factories for textiles, goods and building materials employed hundreds of people. By 1897, the Jewish population reached 5,671; around five hundred Jews earned a livelihood through small trade, and the rest were artisans. The non-Jewish population, about 1,200 in number, was employed mainly in farm work. By 1939, when the war started, Chmielnik's population was 12,500, of which 80 per cent, or 10,275, were Jewish. Because of the Jewish majority, small trade lay in Jewish hands, so that when the stores were closed on Shabbes and *yom tovim*, holidays, one got the impression that the population of Chmielnik was 100 per cent Jewish.

After World War I, the Poalei Zion, a Zionist movement, established the first *Yidishe folks-biblyotek*, the Jewish people's library, which benefited nearly all the young people, from all political streams. Jewish youth were given an opportunity to learn about secular, worldly issues, whether they attended the Polish public schools or the Jewish schools. The Poalei Zion also directed a school called the Borochov Shule, and other Zionist organizations, such as Mizrachi and Agudath Israel, established religious girls' schools, Yavne and Bais Yaakov. Every child was given the opportunity to attend a Jewish school, even if the family did not have the means to pay tuition. Education was a priority for Chmielnik's Jewish population – in comparison to the larger cities in Poland at that time, there was almost no illiteracy in our town.

Between the two world wars, as life in Chmielnik continued at a lethargic pace, our family blossomed. My older sister, Tova Leah, was born in 1917, and I was born two years later. My two younger sisters, Faigele and Rokhelle, were born in 1925 and 1931, respectively. Both my parents had extended family in Chmielnik. My father had been born there, as had my mother.

At the beginning of the 1930s, *hachshara,* or training programs, were formed in various parts of the country; these programs were aimed at the many young men and women who wished to prepare themselves to make aliyah, immigrate, to Palestine. We envied these courageous people who succeeded in tearing themselves away from our monotonous small-town life to become pioneers in a future Jewish state. In some cases, a select few Zionist youth received certificates from the Jewish Agency that permitted them to make aliyah to the land they so longed for. Their parents often forbade them to leave, even though in the early thirties, one could feel in Poland the rebirth of long-entrenched antisemitism. Our town, just like the whole Yiddish-speaking world, closely followed events in Germany after Adolf Hitler was appointed chancellor in 1933.

The world had practically ignored *Mein Kampf* when it was pub-

lished. Written while Hitler was in Landsberg Prison, its main pur-
pose was to poison the German people with hatred of Jewish people.
*Mein Kampf* achieved its aim in Germany, but I felt that the atmo-
sphere also began to change in Poland. The state of the European
economy also played its part, continuing its decline as the Depression worsened. It was easy for the Polish people to assume that it was
the Jew who was responsible for all their *tzores*, their troubles.

The Polish leadership no doubt played its part in the promotion
of antisemitism to the Polish people who, for hundreds of years, had
taken revenge on the Jewish population for every misfortune in the
country. When the first antisemitic laws went into effect in Germany,
such as the boycott law of 1933, which forbade buying from Jewish
shopkeepers, Polish society followed suit in its own way – nationalist
organizations fought against trade with Jews and even physically attacked Jews and Jewish stores. The police did nothing in response to
these fascist gangs.

Gradually, some universities in Poland began to introduce *numerus clausus*, quotas. In 1936, Poland even issued a law prohibiting ko-
sher animal slaughter. When the Jewish deputies in the Sejm, the Polish parliament, protested the rising violence against Jews, a gentile
deputy suggested a compromise: beatings, no, but boycott of Jewish
businesses, yes. Once again, lies from the Middle Ages began to appear, particularly the blood libel, the lie that Jews used the blood of
Christian children in the baking of matzos for Passover. The ground-
work had been laid for anti-Jewish actions. In 1936, a Polish gang brutally attacked innocent Jews in Przytyk, a town just over a hundred
kilometres away. The pogrom caused many Jewish deaths and will
always remain as a shameful stain on the Polish nation. After the pogrom, we lived in fear, lest we be next. During these difficult times,
our life was made even more difficult when my mother died of tuberculosis at only forty-two years old.

In October 1938, Hitler ordered all Jews of Polish extraction out of
Germany and thousands of Jews arrived in Chmielnik from the bor-

der city of Zbąszyń. As the economic situation for the Jewish population of Chmielnik grew precarious, our family decided to move to Lodz, the second-largest industrial city in Poland. We felt we would be safer in a bigger city that had a large Jewish population. In the fall of 1938, my father, my three sisters and I settled in an area of Lodz where other religious Jews also lived. In our building, there were two *bote-medrashim*, houses of prayer and study. There, whole days were spent in the study of the Torah and when Shabbes or *yom tov* arrived, a special holiday mood prevailed in the neighbourhood.

However, the month after we arrived in Lodz, frightening news reached us about the systematic burning of the synagogues throughout Germany during Kristallnacht, the "night of broken glass," when Jewish shops were looted and synagogues torched. To me this was reminiscent of the 1933 fire set to the Reichstag, the parliament, which had given Germany a pretext to arrest political opponents of the Nazi regime, along with many Jews.

It felt as though the Polish-Jewish population was gripped with fear, as well as a premonition that difficult times were coming. At that time, my father underwent major surgery for cancer at the Jewish hospital in Lodz that was named after Izrael Poznański. When I visited him after his surgery, we spoke about the speedy medical intervention and then my father remarked that it was a pity he wasn't allowed to "fall asleep." When I asked him why, he explained that, based on the press reports arriving from Germany and Adolf Hitler's venomous speeches, it was very likely that the Germans were preparing to start a war. Should they be successful in conquering Poland, he expected that the first victims would be the Jews.

# The Sky Ablaze

In March 1938, Hitler's armies marched into Austria; in October, they occupied the Sudetenland, the German-speaking part of Czechoslovakia, in the name of gaining *Lebensraum*, living space, for ethnic Germans. I don't know whether European governments sensed that this was just the beginning, but to me it felt that prior to these events, the world had not reacted to the war psychosis Hitler was igniting in Germany. Hitler was not satisfied with occupying only part of Czechoslovakia – Germany completed its occupation of the country in March 1939. And about six months later, on September 1, 1939, on a sunny Friday morning, the great catastrophe happened: Hitler's Germany attacked Poland. In hindsight, we now know that this was the beginning of the end for the three-and-a-half-million Polish Jews.

That same Friday morning, German airplanes appeared in the skies over the larger Polish cities, spreading death and destruction. The first bombs fell on Warsaw, the Polish capital. Soon, Polish radio broadcast false news from Warsaw, stating that the Polish army had driven away the enemy and was heroically defending every centimetre of Polish soil. Marshal Edward Rydz-Śmigły was reported to have declared on the radio that "not even one button of our uniforms will be forfeited by us to the Germans." Instead, Hitler's planes flew freely in Polish skies, spreading panic among the helpless population. The

Polish military, outfitted with outmoded equipment, could in no way wage war successfully against the modern German war machine.

On Sunday, September 3, England declared war on Germany, but this didn't help the Polish military, which was completely falling apart. Still, the army, small in number, tried to defend the capital and called on Poles throughout the land to come to Warsaw and help in its defence.

As soon as we heard that the German army had crossed the border, we assembled in the *bote-medrashim* in our apartment complex in Lodz and implored God not to allow the enemy to capture Poland. When the call came from Warsaw that all men should come to protect the city, people in Lodz panicked, not knowing what to do. Everyone asked one another for advice. Should we listen to the radio broadcasts appealing to us to help protect the city from the German onslaught? Should we leave home and let our wives and children fend for themselves? Nobody knew what to do.

There were rumours that if the Germans entered Lodz, they would kill all the Jewish men. Finally, many reached the decision that the best thing to do was leave Lodz. Thousands of men, Jewish and non-Jewish, began a massive march to Warsaw, including me. I took only the most essential items, as though I was going out for a walk, and my father stayed in Lodz to take care of my sisters.

Some, perhaps the braver ones, instead of heading for Warsaw, changed direction and marched towards the Bug River in order to continue their way eastward. In August 1939, Germany and the Soviet Union had secretly signed a non-aggression pact by which they had agreed to divide Poland between them. Soon after Germany attacked Poland from the west, the Soviet Union attacked from the east. Many Poles, Jewish and non-Jewish, thought they would be safer in the territories occupied by the Soviet Union.

The stream of travellers on the hundred-kilometre trek from Lodz to Warsaw, as well as from other Polish cities, began as soon as the sun rose on the horizon. The roads and highways were filled with soldiers from the Polish military mixed with the mass of civilians travelling on foot or by horse and wagon. Some of the soldiers rode on horses or on armoured vehicles remaining from World War I. Though we felt the seriousness of the war, the Polish army made a comical impression. It looked like a fly that wanted to do battle with an elephant.

A few days after the outbreak of the war we could see the speed at which the Germans had overtaken the undefended border cities. We couldn't imagine how the weak Polish army would be able to hold off the mechanized German army. Nevertheless, we went along with the national feeling that perhaps it would still be possible to keep the capital from falling into German hands.

After marching for five hours, hungry and tired, I sat down beside the highway to ease my hunger. I hadn't even had the patience to eat breakfast when I left my family. Suddenly, I heard the roar of airplanes. Everyone rejoiced, thinking that the "mighty" Polish air force had arrived and would attack the German army before it reached Warsaw.

The roar of the airplanes was like music as it came closer. People all around me spontaneously started to sing the Polish national hymn, wanting to overcome the sound. There were shouts of, "To są nasze!" (These are ours!) "Long live Poland!" But as the airplanes descended, we recognized the swastikas on their wings – they were Messerschmitts. At that moment, everyone fell silent. Then, we scattered into the wheat fields and fearfully awaited the first attack of the Luftwaffe. The German planes appeared like locusts, firing on the masses of people on the roads. Soldiers and civilians alike were hit, and when the airplanes left after completing their mission, I saw the extent of the destruction. The dead and wounded were all around. A group of soldiers loaded the wounded onto military vehicles and took them to a nearby village. The dead remained where they were.

Exhausted, I dragged myself to a nearby village to cleanse myself from the dust of the long march. Truthfully, after the bombardment, I wanted to go home, but I decided to continue as planned. I was tortured by the thought of a German victory. I had just witnessed the first instance of German aggression upon an innocent population, and it seemed a prelude to the bloody drama that was just beginning on Polish soil.

After a brief rest, I began to move again in the direction of Warsaw. I did not speak with my fellow marchers; we were all lost in our own thoughts. We marched this way for several hours, without a drop of water to quench our thirst or to wash the dust off our bodies. The sun was burning mercilessly and it was hard to move my feet. When we came upon a village, I found a house that Jews lived in, and I asked for a drink of water. That night I, like thousands of others, slept in the fields. At daybreak I woke up relatively refreshed, ready to resume.

It was better to walk in the morning hours because, as if to spite us, it was unusually hot in the afternoons. On the second day the going was somewhat easier because we were getting closer to our destination. In the evening, as we approached Warsaw, we heard the sound of artillery. As we drew closer we realized that units of the German army were already in the city and that remnants of the Polish army were engaged in strong opposition. The civilian population that helped defend the city paid a high price. Ultimately, 25,800 civilians were killed and another 50,000 were wounded. By the time we got there, Warsaw was burning. We couldn't even enter the city, and so once again we slept in a field.

The following morning, the Germans occupied the entire city and the Polish soldiers who were still alive were taken prisoner. The Germans ordered the thousands of people who had arrived in Warsaw from all over Poland to return home. Resigned and exhausted, we were forced to start moving once again. Many villages and towns we passed on our way back were in flames. The night sky, ablaze, was a terrifying sight.

I continued my journey home together with thousands of Poles, Jews and non-Jews alike. Before reaching the city of Brzeziny, we encountered some German SS. They didn't bother anyone with a gentile name or with a non-Jewish appearance, but they did detain quite a number of Jews, including me. They beat every one of us and held us for more than an hour before ordering us to return to our homes. I continued walking for a few hours, tired, hungry and in pain.

When I reached Lodz, I found it, too, occupied by the German army. Very few people could be seen on the streets. Night was falling and, because the Germans had ordered a curfew, it was forbidden to be outdoors. I took the tram, barely managing to reach home in one piece. With my last ounce of strength, I climbed up to the fourth floor of our building and knocked at the door of our apartment. I felt relieved to be reunited with my family. Though they were distressed by my physical condition, we were happy to be together once again.

I was also very happy to see that my girlfriend, Bronka, was with my family. During my absence she had visited my family every day to support them in the hope that we would yet see one another alive. I had met Bronka a year earlier, in 1938, during our family's summer vacation in a place not far from Lodz. She came from a good Jewish family and that year had finished the Lodz *Gymnasium*, high school. We had spent every evening together and our friendship developed to the point that her parents believed that we would have to think seriously about a future together. Man plans and God laughs. With the outbreak of the war, nothing came of our intentions.

My father and I had been working as teachers, but when the Nazis entered Lodz, the school was closed and we became unemployed. Living conditions became more difficult each day. Those who had the money could buy life's necessities. but the majority of people had to stand in line for long hours for the smallest items. Within a few days, everything in the stores was sold out. Many bakeries shut down because of a shortage of flour, and those that still had some flour had lineups that could last a whole day. My sisters and I would rise at dawn and line up, each of us at a different bakery, in order to get a loaf or two of bread. As though this was not enough, we had to be lucky not to be recognized as Jews by our gentile neighbours, who could report us to the SS. There were instances where a Jew, having been reported, would be bloodily beaten.

Over the next couple of months, anti-Jewish laws made our lives increasingly difficult: we had to give up radios and valuables, such as jewellery and fur coats; the so-called *Sperrstunde*, the curfew, restricted our movements; and Jews were prohibited from going on public transit and into city parks. We had to walk in the street, as walking on the sidewalk was forbidden, and Jewish men had to remove their hats if they passed a German. For disobeying the slightest law, there was the threat of beating and death.

We quickly acclimatized to these conditions, thinking that these were just temporary problems that would improve once the German occupiers established themselves. Unfortunately, our situation became unbearable. Many people sought various means to leave Lodz, thinking that perhaps life in the smaller towns and villages would be more humane, that the occupying forces would not use the same methods to brutalize the population there as in the larger cities. It was nearly impossible, however, to leave the city without an official travel permit, but people disregarded the consequences and began to leave Lodz without one. Some were even brave enough to leave their families for the Soviet Union. All left in the hope that the war would soon end and they could return to their homes. No one could imagine otherwise.

In the middle of November 1939, we decided to return to Chmielnik, the city of our birth, where many of my parents' relatives lived. Except for my mother's brother, who lived in France, my mother's entire family was in Chmielnik at that time. My mother was buried there in the town cemetery. We believed it would be better to survive the terrible war among our relatives, who had lived there for generations.

My sister Tova Leah went with me to the German authorities to try to obtain a permit to leave the city. It was still quite dark when we left our fourth-floor apartment and made our way through the snow-covered streets to Poznański Palace, where the Germans had set up an office for Jewish affairs. When we arrived, hundreds of people were already standing in line, waiting for travel permits.

Suddenly, something happened that brought tears to our eyes. The palace was situated opposite one of Lodz's main synagogues, its only Reform temple, where one could hear the best cantors and choirs accompanied by an organist. As we stood watching, a fire broke out and the shul was quickly enveloped in flames. We could not believe that the Germans would do in Poland what they had done in Germany during Kristallnacht almost exactly a year earlier.

The SS kept "order" and made certain that no one could enter the burning building to rescue the *sifrei* Torah, the scrolls. Firemen stood by, ensuring that nothing happened to the neighbouring houses. We found out later that three other prominent synagogues in the city were set on fire at around the same time. This news struck the Jewish population like a bolt of lightning.

We received the travel permits several hours later. When our cousins discovered that we were planning to leave Lodz, they envied us. We stayed for one more day to say goodbye to family, friends and acquaintances. It was very hard for me to leave Bronka, not knowing how long we were going to be away or how long these circumstances would last. Neither of us imagined that this would be our final farewell.

The following day, we each packed a small valise, taking only essential items. We locked our apartment door, took the key with us and headed for the train. After completing the legal formalities to board the train, we found a car for the five of us where we could move around comfortably in a journey we thought would take a few hours, as our hometown was less than two hundred kilometres away. Instead the trip took nearly a whole day and, fearing that someone might recognize us as Jews, we avoided speaking even one word in Yiddish. We were also each wrapped up in our own thoughts, with worries about leaving Lodz and fears about what tomorrow might bring. The train ended up going only as far as Kielce, about 150 kilometres southeast of Lodz. It was evening and without a way of travelling further, we had no choice but to spend the night there. We would have to find some other means of reaching Chmielnik, another thirty-three kilometres away.

Fortunately, my father remembered that he had a friend in Kielce from the days when he had performed in the Yiddish theatre. We stayed with him for the night and the next morning continued on to Chmielnik with a hired horse and wagon. It was a cold November day, and the horse could barely pull a wagon with five passengers. The road was so covered with snow that we had to push the wagon uphill. The trip from Kielce to Chmielnik took six hours. We arrived in town frozen and hungry and went directly to my father's cousin, who owned an inn. That night we met Jews from various Polish cities who, like us, had come to seek a safe haven until the end of the war, which we all hoped would be soon.

The next morning, we went to the cemetery to visit my mother's grave. Later on in the war, I truly envied her for dying in her own bed. We had returned to Chmielnik because we thought that it, like other shtetls, would be exempt from the anti-Jewish laws. But it was not to be – here, too, placards in Polish displayed various restrictions on Jewish travel, making it hard to get around. Every day, the Nazis issued new decrees regulating our activities. By mid-November, every Jew, regardless of age, had to wear an armband with a Star of David on it. Death was still a consequence for not obeying the anti-Jewish decrees.

Fear for our survival dampened any feelings of opposition. The news that Germany was winning on every front of the war made me feel resigned. We settled into a very small room in the home of a distant relative but after a few days realized that even though we were among extended family, it would not be possible for us to wait out the war with them. Bad news kept coming. Our persecution grew worse from day to day. Many Jews were now escaping the cities and coming en masse to the shtetls in the countryside. Hundreds of families who had never before heard of Chmielnik arrived in town.

Since we were unable to find somewhere convenient to live, I decided to seek my luck elsewhere. We also had family in the neighbouring city of Staszów, and it was possible to go there by train without a travel permit. I hoped for a better chance of finding living quarters there. Though it was hard for me to leave my father and my three sisters, I said farewell and set off for Staszów.

# The Storm Approaches

Staszów, like Chmielnik, had a lively Jewish population before the war, with all kinds of Jewish institutions and active Zionist youth movements. When I was a child, my mother told me that her father, my zaide Eliezer, was born in Staszów. I also knew that a cousin on my father's side, Efraim Zyngier, was the head of the Staszów *kehilla*, so I went directly to his home. His family received me very warmly and even advised me to remain in Staszów and perhaps live out the war there. The following day, I planned to visit my great-aunt Hindele, the sister of my zaide Eliezer.

My heart began to pound as I arrived at the home of Aunt Hindele and Uncle Yitzhak Erlikhman. I had no idea what awaited me here. Would they give me a friendly welcome? Would they have any interest at all in talking to me? This was my first meeting with relatives whom I did not know at all. When I knocked at the door, a little old woman stood before me, her face wrinkled, smiling. As soon as I told her who I was, she started to cry. I can't describe the warm reception I received. We sat for hours and talked about the current situation and family news, as well as about the shortage of living space in Chmielnik.

My aunt told me to bring my family immediately, and that she would share her none-too-large place with us. We would occupy her bedroom and Auntie and Uncle would live in the kitchen. Two days later, convinced my family should settle there, I travelled back to Chmielnik. We decided to accept Aunt Hindele's invitation and a few days later, my father, my three sisters and I once again set out on our way.

My aunt Hindele and my uncle Yitzhak were in their eighties. He was very religious and my aunt was just the opposite. She maintained the household in the Jewish manner that her husband wanted, but in town it was known that she did it just to please her husband, for *shalom bayit*, peace in the home. While Uncle Yitzhak learned Torah daily, Aunt Hindele read books by Dostoyevsky or Sholokhov in her free time. They had three sons in the United States, a daughter in South America, a daughter in Staszów, a son in Palestine and another daughter in the Soviet Union. Influenced by their mother's indifference to religious education, they had all been active during their youth in various political parties.

I remembered that when I was much younger, a cousin from Staszów had come to say goodbye before leaving for Palestine. This was Aunt Hindele's son Getzl Erlikhman. As a member of Hashomer Hatzair, he was one of the founders of Ein Shemer kibbutz in Palestine. I also remember one of Aunt Hindele's daughters, Sorche, who used to visit Chmielnik back in 1925 and 1926, on summer outings with Hashomer Hatzair.

Sorche became involved in the Communist Party during the Piłsudski era in the mid-1920s, when belonging to the Communist Party was illegal. She was arrested several times and put in jail, but when she was set free, she again resumed her political work. Once, when Sorche came back to Staszów from Warsaw, where she worked as a teacher, the police surrounded her parents' house. My aunt Hindele disguised Sorche and helped her escape through a window on the first floor.

When the war erupted, Sorche was in prison in Warsaw. When the Germans attacked the Polish capital, the prisons were opened and she fled to the Soviet Union, where she survived the war. In 1946 or

1947, she returned with her husband, whom she had married in the Soviet Union, and then went to Brazil. Years later she moved to Israel.

We settled in our aunt's place with great difficulty. The conditions were not the best, and the bedroom wasn't very comfortable for five people. Still, we accepted everything lovingly. We were happy to at least have a roof over our heads, but one problem still remained: how could one earn a living? There was a good communal structure in Staszów, with a soup kitchen and clothing collection for those who needed assistance. Their number grew from day to day as our situation worsened, with the anti-Jewish laws becoming even more restrictive. The German military ruled harshly. After sunset, it was forbidden to go outside. Jewish men caught on the street were taken for forced labour or to be tortured. Most painful was to witness how the Nazis treated Jewish men with beards. First they ordered them to cut them off and then, if a Jew was found still wearing a beard, the Germans ripped the beard off by hand.

Soon after the German military entered a city, they closed all Jewish schools, so the children were just idle. Since my father and I had been teachers in Lodz, seeing the children wandering around broke our hearts. That gave me an idea: even though it was against the law, I would gather a few children in my place and carry on their interrupted studies with them. The children would be occupied, and I would earn some money to feed my family.

My father was very pleased with my idea. I put my plan into action, acquiring school textbooks in Polish and Yiddish, in subjects such as history and mathematics. With my aunt's help, we found students and within a few weeks I was able to organize three classes, totalling sixty children. As the number of students grew, our living quarters became so crowded that we had to rent a room not far from where we were living in order to continue our work.

I loved teaching; it gave me a sense of accomplishment. I was so engrossed in the work that I sometimes forgot we were living in a time of terrible war, a war with unforeseen consequences.

~

News arrived from Lodz that the Germans had established a ghetto in February 1940 and ordered that all Jews move there, into a part of the city that was too crowded even for the Jews who had lived there before the war. By May 1, 1940, exactly eight months after the outbreak of the war, the ghetto was sealed off, with 164,000 Jews inside. Transports of Jews were brought there from Berlin, Vienna and Prague.

The Lodz ghetto was completely isolated from the outside world and heavily guarded, making it nearly impossible to escape. The slightest attempt could mean death. Homes that had been left outside of the ghetto, including ours, were confiscated by the Germans or taken over by the Polish population.

At first, I received letters from Bronka about the dreadful situation in the ghetto; her family of eight was living in one room, dying of hunger. Later the letters were censored, and I had to become an expert at reading between the lines. Unfortunately, I was in no position to help her, and I felt hopeless. Our correspondence continued until the Nazis decided to cut off all contact with the ghetto. Though I waited for another letter, none came. I did not hear another word, and I don't know what happened to Bronka and my other friends.

We also had no idea what had happened to the Parizers, our cousins who were born and raised in Lodz. They had a factory where sweaters were made and had employed a considerable number of workers, but immediately after the outbreak of war, the Germans confiscated the factory and the business. We were sure that the entire family of eight had gone into the Lodz ghetto when, out of the blue, we received a letter in 1941, indicating that they were in the Warsaw ghetto, which had been set up in October 1940. Our cousins asked that we do everything possible to find living quarters for them because their circumstances were growing worse from day to day. Jews from nearby cities, towns and villages in Poland were being sent to the ghetto, and death from sickness and hunger was spreading in epidemic proportions.

The day I read the letter I paid a visit to Efraim Zyngier who, as president of the Staszów Jewish community, I hoped could do something for our mutual cousins. My intervention was fruitful, and in a few days a room was ready for the whole family. It would not be easy for them to escape from the Warsaw ghetto, which was tightly guarded by the SS as well as the Polish police, but it was possible to bribe the police. Somehow our cousins managed to escape, and we rejoiced greatly when they arrived in Staszów. Their presence gave us hope that together we would all live through this gruesome time.

The newly arrived family consisted of three men, two women and a one-year-old girl. Two brothers had left for the Soviet Union instead of coming with them. One of the new arrivals, my cousin David, who was named after the same zaide as I was, looked fully "Aryan" because he was blond and had a flat nose, which he had gotten as a boxer in pre-war Poland. David also spoke fluent German because of his *Volksdeutsche* friends. Thanks to his Aryan appearance, he could walk about freely without wearing the Star of David symbol. He was, by nature, a gentle and caring man, always ready to help a fellow Jew in need.

In the summer of 1941, the German press was reporting that various workshops were being set up in Poland to manufacture necessities for the German army, which was now fighting deep inside the Soviet Union. Such workshops, which included ones for making uniforms and other clothes, were even set up in the Warsaw ghetto. Getting a job in a clothing factory seemed the best guarantee for surviving the war.

In Staszów, we still believed that the storm wouldn't affect us. I was so engrossed in my teaching, happy that the children were at least getting some kind of an education, that it was hard to believe that our situation could change so quickly. But in June 1942, a ghetto was established in our small town, too.

My cousin David was brave enough to travel to Krakow – though of course hiding the fact that he was a Jew – and went right to the office of the German governor-general, Hans Frank. David was received twice by officials and was successful in getting a permit to establish a tailoring shop in the Staszów ghetto, capable of employing hundreds of people. This shop opened in Staszów on July 1, 1942, to supply uniforms for the German army; we hoped that it would help save at least some of Staszów's Jewish population.

We kept hearing news that the Germans were sending young men and women to various camps. We heard that transports from the Lodz ghetto were going to places from which they did not return. Naturally, it was hard to believe that all these rumours were true. The Yiddish language was becoming "enriched" with new German words, such as *Umsiedlung*, resettlement, *Umerziehung*, re-education, and other similar words that, in reality, all meant death. Still, no one wanted to believe that the Nazis were planning to murder all of European Jewry. There was hope that the world would not allow such a massive catastrophe, that this was just a passing storm and that the country of Goethe and Schiller would be unable to carry out the intentions of Hitler and his henchmen.

From Warsaw, we soon received reports that the Judenrat, the Jewish Council, had to supply the Germans with the names of hundreds of families for "resettlement." Near the end of July, we learned that the head of the Warsaw Judenrat, Adam Czerniaków, had committed suicide, knowing the future that lay in store for the masses of deportees.

Two months later, we heard that the first "resettlement" of the Jews in Staszów would soon occur. This news caused panic. We knew what this meant. Our only hope was to get into one of the tailor shops. But how could thousands be employed when there was room for only hundreds? And what would happen to the children? The Judenrat worked feverishly, day and night, to hire as many families as possible.

Though we felt helpless, we used whatever pull we had with the Judenrat to save our families from certain death. On September 12, the first day of Rosh Hashanah, my father, my three sisters and I went to our cousin Efraim Zyngier and his family to wish them a good year. We had a long talk about the developing issues and, of course, asked Efraim to engage the five of us in the tailor shop so that we would have a chance of surviving. Efraim told us the Germans had requested that a few hundred young people be supplied to work in a munitions plant at Skarżysko-Kamienna, where they would apparently work under the best conditions. Naturally, the production of ammunition was very important for the German war machine, and so there was a possibility that those who volunteered for Skarżysko-Kamienna would remain there until the end of the war.

Our cousin promised us that my father and three sisters would find a place in the tailoring shops if I volunteered at the Judenrat for Skarżysko. Efraim was concerned that he not appear to be looking after everyone in his family. We reluctantly agreed with his suggestion, said farewell to our cousin and went home to prepare for what was to come.

During the night, various thoughts bothered me, thoughts that would not let me fall asleep. How would my father be able to manage with the three children? And I? Should I leave my family to save my life and work in the munitions factory, where good working conditions were promised? Not having any other choice, the following morning I went to the office of the Staszówer Judenrat, and together with a few hundred men and women, signed up to leave for Skarżysko-Kamienna.

# Fighting the Fear

On October 10, 1942, the day I left with my transport for Skarżysko-Kamienna, I said farewell to my students and to my dear Aunt Hindele and Uncle Yitzhak. My uncle couldn't sense the danger of the hour because his health was failing. When the moment came to say goodbye to my father and sisters, we all started crying. I was overcome with mixed feelings of hope and resignation, but I would never have imagined that we were saying goodbye for the last time.

In the marketplace, near the house of the Judenrat, trucks for the volunteers were idling. An armed SS guard stood in each truck. We boarded the trucks and once again waved farewell, unable to utter a word as we choked back tears. As the trucks started to move, I now had the feeling that we were parting from our loved ones forever. The trucks were so crowded that we had to travel standing up. We drove along damaged roads for five hours, without a drop of water or morsel of food, until we reached Skarżysko-Kamienna in the evening.

None of us had any idea what awaited us in this German-promised "Garden of Eden." We didn't imagine that we were coming for a rest, but we believed that we would be working in relatively humane conditions because the Germans needed us to produce ammunition. Yet as soon as we got off the truck we were faced by Ukrainian *Werkschutz*, security guards, in black uniforms who greeted us with blows and swore at us. The guards led us into a large hall. Soon the SS-

*Obersturmführer* appeared and ordered us to hand over everything of value, such as gold, silver, watches and money. We were warned that anyone later found with these possessions would be shot.

When the Nazis first organized the so-called work camps, or La-ger, they recruited Jewish police from among the workers, giving them the job of keeping order in the work camp itself. These Jewish policemen went around collecting all the valuables after the *Ober-sturmführer*'s "welcome." This spectacle lasted for a few hours as clothes that had valuables sewn into them were ripped apart. People had hoped to use these valuables to save lives but now watched as the items were thrown into containers. We were given a drink of water late in the evening but were not allowed any food. I didn't even feel hungry, due to the fear that stirred within me.

From the Jewish police we found out that Skarżysko-Kamienna held the largest munitions plant in Poland and that thousands of Pol-ish workers were employed in the factories. There were three camps, Werke A, B and C, in different parts of the city. After World War I, the factories in Skarżysko had become the property of a German in-dustrial firm, Hugo Schneider Aktiengesellschaft (HASAG). As early as 1939, Jews had been employed as temporary workers, but the first Jewish prisoners were brought here in March 1942. Now the camps produced war machinery with forced labour, Jewish slaves.

An SS officer told us to line up in a row with our baggage and informed us that we were going to Werk C. Since we had arrived at night, we could barely make out the distant, lit-up wooden barracks of Werk C through the dark forest. When we were led in through the gate to the Lager, I could see that the place was surrounded by a few rows of barbed wire and armed guards in watchtowers. We were all extremely frightened. There was no way back.

It was so dark that we couldn't see the condition of the barracks. After being assigned a place to sleep, I, like everyone else, simply col-lapsed, dead tired, on a wooden plank and fell asleep, fully clothed. It was only in the morning that I saw where we were: Werk C consisted of about twenty wooden barracks where men and women lived separately. The sanitary conditions were primitive – one barrack served as a toilet and washroom, with only cold water for washing and other needs. There was also a medical section, without medicine. At best the doctors could treat patients with pills for toothaches or headaches.

The only "comfortable" barrack was the so-called White House, in which three families lived – the children and grandchildren of Frau Gutman, a widow who had lived with her large family in relatively good conditions in the town of Skarżysko until 1941. I learned later that after the Wannsee Conference of January 1942, when the Nazis first openly articulated their devilish plan of total elimination of the Jewish population, the Nazis and their Ukrainian and Lithuanian helpers carried out the mass deportation of the Jewish population of Skarżysko. The extended Gutman family, however, managed to avoid the fate of the Skarżysko Jews. As soon as the Werk C Lager was opened, the three families willingly moved in with all their possessions and, thanks to their material influence, were successful in taking over the administration of the Lager; like the Judenräte in the ghettos, they enforced all laws and orders applying to the prisoners.

Frau Fela Markowiczowa, Frau Gutman's daughter, became the *Kommandantin*, carrying out all the German orders in the hope of saving herself, her six-year-old daughter and the other members of her family. One of her brothers-in-law, Henek Eisenberg, took over the administration of the Jewish *Ordnungsdienst*, the ghetto police, while a second took over distribution of the *Verpflegung*, provisions.

The daily food ration consisted of two hundred grams of sticky bread, a cup of artificial coffee and a watery soup. Working conditions were not easy. We were awakened at 5:00 a.m. and had to line up within a quarter of an hour for a cup of fake coffee. It was impossible to wash or even go to the bathroom. Half an hour later we had to march to work in military fashion, accompanied by the Ukrainian *Werkschutz*, guards, and Jewish police. Each group was led to its own section and worked twelve hours a day, every day but Sunday.

When our group from Staszów arrived at Werk C, the Lager was in full swing. Hundreds of men and women from various cities were already there. Some had arrived only five months earlier, yet they could barely stand on their feet and their bodies were so emaciated from starvation that they were hardly recognizable. They told us terrible things, that the beatings and working conditions were unbearable. We learned that some had attempted to run away and though a few had succeeded, those caught by the Germans or Ukrainians were immediately shot. Many had died from the inhumane conditions – the terrible filth and hunger, the hard labour.

That very week I met two of my cousins who had arrived from Chmielnik a few weeks earlier. Already they looked pitiful, and I never saw them again. A few days later the Germans made a *selekcja*, selection, and took all the weak and sick inmates away. Eventually we found out that they were transported by truck a few kilometres from the Lager and shot. Such selections took place very often, as the Nazis considered this the best method for curing all kinds of sicknesses in order to avoid an epidemic that might harm the German and Ukrainian guards. The resulting death rate was massive.

The HASAG factories in Werk C produced grenades, bombs, underwater mines, ammunition and bullets for all kinds of military machinery. Two yellow-coloured chemicals, Trotyl (TNT) and picric acid, were used in the production of bombs and mines. These substances were so harmful to one's health, especially to the lungs, that before the war, employees in the munitions factories worked only three hours a day, wore masks and rubber gloves and had to drink a glass of milk hourly to neutralize the toxic effects. Even now the gentile workers wore white elastic gloves. In general, the conditions for the Polish gentiles were quite different from those of the Jews. They came to work well rested and well fed, were paid for their work and worked fewer hours.

Since we Jews were not given masks or gloves, the dust from the chemical substances penetrated our noses and mouths so that there was always a bitter taste in our mouths; even the soup and the bread we ate tasted bitter. But the worst off were the men and women who worked at producing underwater mines. The *Hallen*, or workshops, 11, 13 and 15 manufactured bombs made of picric acid. This chemical substance was even more bitter than Trotyl and was not only harmful to one's health, but caused one's clothing to take on a yellow colour and fall apart. The acid penetrated all parts of the body and its yellow colour was impossible to get rid of. The people in these factories looked like scarecrows; in the camp lexicon, a skinny, skeletal person was called a *Muselmann*.

I was assigned to work in *Halle* 53, where fifty-kilogram artillery shells were produced. We Jewish prisoners worked side by side with the gentile workers, many of whom showed little interest in our fate. I tried to establish a good relationship with them in the hope that some of them would feel some humanity for us, the victims of German hatred. A few showed some understanding of our circumstances and secretly shared a bit of food. Most, though, used their contact with us for their own interest, selling us products in exchange for the clothes that we wore.

The beginning of the winter of 1942 was very severe. The barracks were heated with wood, which was hard to get. I was lucky to have brought a warm coat from home. One cold morning, a gentile worker offered to buy the coat from me in exchange for food, saying that I wouldn't need it for long anyhow. I made the exchange, satisfying my hunger for a while. The same thing happened with my leather shoes, which still looked half-decent to her. She proposed that I accept several loaves of bread in exchange for the shoes. It was difficult for me to get another pair of shoes, but when a transport of clothes arrived, I managed to get a pair of shoes with wooden soles. I then gave the woman my leather shoes for bread, and once again rescued myself from hunger.

Some worried about their own skin and took no note of neighbours or friends, a result of the Nazi plan to systematically rid Jewish inmates of all human feeling. After robbing us of everything we owned, the Germans persecuted us at every turn, deadening our feelings and, finally, killing us through work, starvation and disease. Under these conditions, it was very easy to despair. I overcame this feeling by gathering around me a circle of friends who had been brought here at the same time. Every evening after work we would get together in one of the barracks to share news, whether true or false. Sometimes we got a newspaper from the gentile workers and followed the news of the war, but the best method we had of overcoming our fears and resignation was to gather every Sunday for a few hours to sing. Through this, we were able to forget where we were.

Our singing circle became so popular that we had to arrange these Sunday sessions outdoors, as the number of participants kept growing. Everyone longed for some culture and human warmth, and in spite of the difficult circumstances of the week, we all waited impatiently for Sunday.

The musical Sundays soon became a cultural gathering with the participation of a number of talented men and women. We conducted the concerts in two languages, Yiddish and Polish. Not only prisoners came to performances but also the leaders of the Lager, including Fela Markowiczowa, who never missed a concert.

～

We found out from our gentile co-workers that massive deportations of the Jewish population were taking place in nearly all the cities of Poland and that this included Staszów. I was distressed that I hadn't remained with my family to share their destiny and was sleepless for many nights. I couldn't stop thinking about my father and three sisters, especially the youngest, Rokhelle, barely eleven years old. We knew by then that "resettlement" meant deportation to the death camps of Auschwitz or Treblinka. I desperately hoped that my family could survive in the tailor shops that had been organized a few months before, thanks to my cousin David Parizer.

I was restless. Could I escape from the Lager and be reunited with my family? I spoke to a man from Lwów who also sought to run away. He came up with a plan: he spoke Ukrainian and had befriended a Ukrainian who was willing to let us through the gate for a sum of money. I found myself in a dilemma. First of all, where would I get the money? Second, what guarantee did we have that he wouldn't shoot us after letting us out? Third, how would I manage to get to Staszów? These questions plagued me day and night. I was unable to reach a conclusion, and then fate intervened to make this plan come to nothing.

When we returned to the Lager from work one cold, snowy day, I felt so weak that I could hardly stand. I made my way to the sick *Revier*, station, where the doctor told me that I had typhus. When I asked what could be done, the doctor said that he had no medicines, so I would have to go to Barrack 7, where all those suffering from typhus were quarantined in order to to keep the epidemic from spreading.

Because of the shortage of medicine, the epidemic had spread anyhow, so that when I went into Barrack 7 nearly all the beds were occupied. There were about sixty men and women there, and the only place free was on the top level of the three-tiered wooden bunks. I climbed up and collapsed on the hard board.

Fearful of contamination, very few of my friends came to inquire about my condition. I could not get down from the bunk without help, nor could I take off or put on my wooden shoes because my feet were so swollen, and so I had to rely on the sanitation workers for help with my physiological needs. I couldn't swallow bread or even soup, and I survived only on the warm tea that *Kommandantin* Markowiczowa sent to me because she knew me from the Sunday musical concerts. Apparently I was luckier than others, who didn't even get tea. I lay there helpless, getting worse from day to day. My fever kept rising and I was unconscious for two days. I lost my desire to live and didn't even react to the suffering and screams of the other patients.

We knew from the news that reached us from various sources that the Nazi methods of murder were pitiless, but we didn't think that they would use these methods against us at a time when they needed slave labourers for the production of munitions. Yet, at dawn one Sunday I was awakened by the voices of other patients. A transport truck carrying SS officers had arrived at Barrack 7. The SS ordered all the sick to come down from their bunks and forced them, with blows, onto the truck. As soon as I saw their uniforms I instinctively, with my last bit of strength, pried away some boards on the ceiling that were not nailed down. I climbed behind, replaced the boards and lay there with my heart beating fast, terrified that the Nazis would hear it.

I soon heard hysterical cries together with orders shouted in German. "Schneller machen!" (Hurry up!) I could have been discovered at any moment, and would have had to share the fate of all the sick ones. I was sure that the soldiers were taking us away to be killed. Right then, truth to tell, I had no fear of being shot. Maybe my unhealthy condition kept me from fully understanding the consequences. The only thing I worried about was my family in Staszów. How would they know how I had perished and where my bones were?

I heard steps approaching. I was afraid that this was a Nazi murderer, but then I heard a familiar voice and saw a man in civilian clothes holding a lantern. I calmed down as he looked up at me and spoke my name in Polish. It was the sanitation worker, Alek, who was supposed to help evacuate all the sick in Barrack 7. He told me that *Kommandantin* Markowiczowa had sent him to rescue me from the transport, since everyone on it was going to be shot. He led me to a different exit into the other half of Barrack 7, where the factory night workers lived. They had not yet returned from work. He set me down on a *Pritsche*, a pallet, and covered me with straw, telling me to remain motionless until the transport truck with the sick ones left. As I lay there, covered with straw, I imagined the Nazis and *Werkschutz* lining up all the sick, including me, to be shot. When I finally heard that the truck had left with its victims, I was extremely relieved. In my heart, I thanked my rescuers for saving my life.

About an hour later I crawled out and slowly left Barrack 7, still worrying that a German or Ukrainian might spot me. After lying in bed for ten days, and still feverish, I could hardly move, and the high snow around the barracks did not make movement easier. Finally, I dragged myself to my barrack and lay down.

I managed to get permission to remain in the barrack for another few days, which helped me to regain my strength. Gradually, we resumed our Sunday evening concerts, which had been discontinued because of my illness.

~

Among those who had arrived with the group from Staszów were my close friend Hirsh Tochterman and his brother Yitzhak, who came from a prominent family. Hirsh hadn't completed university but was very capable and had taught himself how to play violin. Beyond this, he had a special inclination for languages. When I became acquainted with him in 1940, Hirsh was fluent in six languages. His desire to educate himself in the little shtetl, with limited means, was amazing.

Thanks to our musical Sundays, we were invited to an evening with the *Kommandantin*. She suggested that Hirsh teach English to her six-year-old daughter and to the seven-year-old daughter of her sister. This would free him from work in the munitions plant, and he would get paid. Naturally, Hirsh immediately agreed.

My health gradually improved, and I returned to my hard labour in *Halle* 53. The leader of our section was a long-time employee, Stefan Biernatski, who had a tolerant attitude and was even friendly to some of the Jewish forced labourers. On the other hand, his helper, Antek, was a thirty-year-old peasant who walked around with a thick stick and lashed out at a different victim every day. On the pretext that someone wasn't working hard enough or that the quality wasn't up to standard, Antek would choose someone to pick on and beat him unmercifully. None of our gentile co-workers interfered for fear that someone would report them to the German supervisor, who visited us daily.

Still, I met a few humane gentiles. One was Vatslav Gastomski, a resident of Skarżysko who had been working in the same section for ten years. Every day, we met in the bathroom and he relayed the latest news to me, keeping me up to date on the course of the war. He even brought me clippings from an underground newspaper, which I shared with my friends, as well as food. We had to be careful that none of the Germans or even the other Polish co-workers found out about this.

I remained worried about the fate of my family. We kept hearing more news of deportations to camps, places of total annihilation. I asked Gastomski to go to Staszów and contact my father, as well as other families of the prisoners confined in Werk C, and promised to reward him if he succeeded in bringing letters and money from them. He agreed, although this was no easy matter. He had to have a reason for leaving work, as the Germans administered heavy punishment to those who were absent without a good reason. However, they accepted his letter from a doctor, and my friend left for Staszów with my letter, along with a number of letters I had gathered from other prisoners.

I worried about him until he returned to work a few days later and brought me a pack of letters. I could hardly wait to see a letter from my family. I prayed to God that the Germans or Ukrainians wouldn't discover the pack of letters during check-in at the gate. When I returned safely to my barrack with the letters in hand, our mood was celebratory. A spark of hope was kindled that we would live through this nightmare and be reunited with our families. With trembling hands I opened the letter from my father:

*My dear David! It is already so long since you left us. We have never stopped crying about being separated. We worry very much about your well-being. We know from the messenger that you were sick with typhus and that you work very hard. We greatly regret that you went away voluntarily at the advice of Efraim Zyngier. If only you would have re-*

*mained together with us, then maybe you would also have been saved to work in the tailoring shop. For the time being we are still in our own location. It's possible that we will be transferred to the tailoring workshop next week, but we won't know what will happen with us until then because massive deportations are taking place from the surrounding cities. There are rumours circulating that everyone is being taken to their death. I hope that this is just propaganda. I'm overjoyed that you found a way to connect with us. Presently we feel relatively well but who knows what awaits us. I'm enclosing twenty złotys, with which I hope you will be able to buy something. Warm regards and kisses from your sisters Tova, Faigele and Rokhelle. I kiss you warmly, my dear son.*

As I read this letter, I sobbed bitterly. That night, I couldn't fall asleep. My conscience bothered me for leaving Staszów, but there was no way to change my decision. I continued to go to work every day, marching, standing in line for a bit of bread and enduring Antek's brutal behaviour. One time he picked on me and beat me with his thick stick. One had to give him gifts in order to avoid his beatings, so with ten złotys I managed to buy time until my turn came again.

Not long after, I found another opportunity to ask my friend Gastomski to go once again to Staszów with a package of letters. He went there only to find that things had changed completely. On November 8, 1942, a few days before his arrival, the liquidation had taken place. The SS and their Ukrainian helpers had dragged nearly the entire Jewish population – men, women and children – out of their homes and assembled them, with unmerciful blows, in the large marketplace.

He heard that the first victim of this gruesome evacuation was my cousin, the head of the *kehilla*, Efraim Zyngier; his wife, Faigele, had been murdered a few days earlier. The weak and the sick, those who were unable to go quickly to the assembly points, were also shot. The Nazis forced thousands to march to the nearest train station for the journeys to Treblinka and Belzec, leaving behind hundreds of dead.

And so our messenger did not bring any letters, just the tragic news of what had happened, leaving us dumbfounded.

The only good news was that the Nazis had spared the lives of the few hundred Jews in the tailoring workshops. Among these fortunate ones were my father and three sisters.

A few weeks later my friend Gastomski again travelled to Staszów to bring letters from the few who had miraculously survived in the tailoring workshops. This time, my father's letter was brief, tragic because of the bloody events that had taken place a few weeks before. He wrote that not only had our cousins Efraim and his wife been killed, but also that my aunt and uncle, the Erlikhmans, were gone. For the time being, the shop workers were safe, but no one knew for how long. There was even talk, my father wrote, that the Germans were planning to transfer everyone to a newly established work camp in Poniatowa. He added that a room had been assigned to him and the three girls, which would be shared with a couple. This couple came to Staszów from a city called Kalisz and their only son, Natek Neugarten, was in the same Lager as me. My father asked me to do everything I possibly could to lighten our hopeless situation.

That very day, I learned that Natek was in my barrack. He was so happy to hear the contents of my father's letter, and from that moment on I felt a responsibility towards my new friend. During our first conversation I found out that Natek came from a partly assimilated family. His father had owned a large business, and Natek had graduated from university in the summer of 1939. I sought every means to ease our suffering. Through my connections at the camp, I arranged for us to work in the same factory, and we shared any bread we got. To protect ourselves from the harsh frost, we used the paper sacks the chemical supplies came in, as we had no winter clothing.

Though it had been only two months since our arrival, many of our group from Staszów had already died from hunger, hard work and illness. The infirmary had doctors and aides, but without medicine they could not do anything more than grant a permit to leave the factory for a day or two.

Meanwhile, reports continued to arrive about the annihilation of the Jewish population in the ghettos, as the "resettlement" to the concentration camps increased in tempo. We knew from the tragic news that reached us that all the small shtetls in the Kielce region had been liquidated. I heard that Jews remained only in the larger ghettos of Lodz and Warsaw. We knew that some resistance against the Nazis had occurred in various camps and ghettos, but the hunger and the difficult working conditions here deadened any motivation for an uprising. All we wanted was to survive the day.

A couple of weeks had passed since the last letters we'd received through my friend Gastomski. On the day of my mother's *yahrzeit*, I was seized by a terrible longing for my family. I had a feeling that something had happened to my father and three sisters. My friend Gastomski agreed to travel once more before the Germans transferred the shops to the planned work camps in Poniatowa.

I collected a number of letters and gave them to Gastomski one Friday afternoon, praying in my heart for him to find our loved ones. The next day, Shabbes morning, when we lined up in rows of five, ready to march off to work, the Jewish *Ordnungsdienst* gave us the good news that twice monthly, every second Sunday, we would be able to go to the bath in Werk A. This was a surprise for all of us, especially for those who had been in the Lager for two years and had to wash, both summer and winter, with cold water.

All the prisoners gathered joyfully to go bathe for the first time. Our mood remained festive despite being guarded by armed Ukrainians for the whole march. This was the first time that we had had an opportunity to meet with the men and women from the other Lager and share our experiences. After the warm bath, we hoped that things would continue to change for the better. Even nature seemed to rejoice with us because the sun suddenly started to shine on this cold December day, and it warmed our shattered bodies as we marched back to Werk C.

The concert that evening maintained our sense of hope. I prepared a program suited to the mood of the hundreds of attendees and paid little attention to the presence of German and Ukrainian workers who might have understood Yiddish or Polish. This may have been naïve on my part, since I included in the program songs and sketches that the Germans could interpret as anti-Nazi propaganda, but thankfully the evening passed without any surprises.

That night, I couldn't fall asleep, knowing that the following day I might receive word from my family; however, my friend did not come to work until a day later than expected. I met him again in the toilet to get the pack of letters. He told me that the situation concerning the tailoring shops was very serious. Though Gastomski had managed to enter the heavily guarded centre, he was able to stay only one hour, so he saw only a few people who gave him letters and money. It appeared, he told me, that all the people and machinery were soon to be moved. As soon as we got back to the barracks, I distributed the letters and read my father's letter.

*My dear son David! I was so happy to receive from the honoured messenger your letter and living proof of your existence in the Lager. It's too bad, though, that your friend couldn't spend much time with us. We are already packed and ready to leave Staszów. We are promised that we are headed for a Lager in Poniatowa, near Lublin, where we will live and work in good conditions. Truthfully I don't have any trust in these promises after what happened to the rest from Staszów. Unfortunately I must write you that your sister Tova Leah fell sick with tuberculosis and we have no ability to treat her here. I have to keep this a secret because no one must know, or it could cost her her life. Faigele and Rokhelle feel as can be expected under the circumstances. I hope that we will be in contact from Poniatowa. I end with warm kisses and with the hope that we will shortly be together. Your father, Itche.*

I wept when I read this letter and worried about my father and sisters all night long. I feared that the deportation from Staszów to Poniatowa was to be the last journey that my family would take.

# Would That I Had Never Known This Place

In early 1943, a typhus epidemic spread through the Lager with exceptional speed. I was grateful that I had already gone through a bout of typhus and therefore could move about freely, without fear of being infected again. Once again, the Germans issued a strict order that anyone suspected of suffering from typhus be isolated immediately in Barrack 7. Among those affected was my friend Hirsh Tochterman. After five days in Barrack 7 with a high fever, he died.

Because of the shortage of Jewish workers, production in the munitions factory dropped. Antek went around with his thick stick, attacking the workers who had not yet been infected. Even the gentile factory workers avoided contact with us. The deaths meant the loss of hundreds of friends and acquaintances; we never knew where their bones were buried and could not even say Kaddish at their graves. We knew that the Germans would kill all the sick. Every Sunday morning at dawn the SS transport truck picked up sick patients from Barrack 7 to be shot. The tragedy was even greater when a child was taken away. Throughout the whole Lager we heard the screams of those sentenced to death. I felt so much empathy for them and yet could do nothing. There was only one thing to do: continue working as long as our legs held us up.

In mid-January, a transport of new prisoners arrived at Skarżysko; they were sent to the HASAG munitions factory to replace workers lost to the typhus outbreak. A friend from my hometown, Alter, was among the new arrivals. Alter told me about his experiences in the Chmielnik ghetto before its liquidation, describing in detail how the Germans and their Ukrainian helpers had gathered the whole Jewish population in the large market and brutally murdered the old, the sick and the young children. He also told me that my entire extended family, all sixty of them, including all the children, were among the dead. I could not stop thinking about the terrifying fate of these innocents.

Alter explained how he had ended up in Skarżysko after fleeing from Chmielnik. On December 1, 1942, news had spread of German- and Polish-language bulletins stating that a Jewish quarter was being established in Sandomierz, east of Kielce, and that Jews who applied by a certain date would not have to fear deportation. The governor, Hans Frank, even signed a statement that the Jews would be able to live there without hindrance until the end of the war, so many Jewish families did indeed respond to this plan.

Jews came from well-concealed hiding places, even those who could have passed as gentiles. The Nazis set up everything perfectly, immediately establishing an autonomous Judenrat, a Jewish committee, and even permitting Jews to do business with the surrounding gentile population. Pictures of the new *Judenstaat*, the Jewish "state," were published in the press for propaganda purposes. But the Jews had made a colossal error. The Germans had an annihilation plan in place. When, after a few weeks, no more Jews came forward, the Germans surrounded the city. On the evening of January 10, 1943, they carted all the men, women and children away by horse and wagon to the train station where freight trains were waiting. They sent all the healthy men and women to work in Skarżysko, Alter among them, and loaded the remainder into sealed cattle cars to be sent to the gas chambers of Treblinka.

~

In the spring of 1943, more terrifying news arrived: thousands of Jews had been deported from Warsaw to the gas chambers of Treblinka. On April 19, 1943, a group of brave Jews had risen up against the Nazis in an attempt to resist deportation. The Warsaw ghetto was ultimately set ablaze by the Nazis, and those who survived were sent to Treblinka, to Majdanek or to forced labour camps. Even so, news of the Warsaw Ghetto Uprising lifted our moods. We marvelled at the courage of these heroic ghetto fighters, even though we could not emulate them. Much of our opposition was passive, with acts of sabotage, such as a few bomb explosions in Werke A and C.

I did hear of some Jewish workers who conspired against our enemy. This was thanks to Kowalik, the Polish boss in Werk C's Schmitz section, who was a member of the Armia Krajowa, the underground Polish anti-Nazi movement. The Schmitz section was considered among the better places to work because Jews were treated decently there, and some of the workers were able to smuggle ammunition and various weapons out of the factory; they also secretly got money that made it possible to buy essential articles from the Polish workers. They were limited in how much they could do – if the Germans had found out about this activity it would have ended in tragedy. As far as I know, this work was carried out right to the end without victims, although there were rumours, later, that Kowalik was arrested in the summer of 1944.

In June 1943, around one hundred young men and women arrived at Werk C. They were first sent from the Warsaw ghetto to Majdanek near Lublin, but because of the shortage of workers in Skarżysko they were transported here to replace the hundreds who had perished. From them we learned how the Nazis destroyed the occupants of the Warsaw ghetto. Much later, we would hear about the liquidation of the Lodz ghetto, too, in the summer of 1944, when people were sent to Chełmno and Auschwitz.

Among the newcomers from Majdanek were a few doctors who were put to work in the sick house. There were also some singers and actors, as well as the writer Mordechai Strigler, thanks to whom the Sunday concerts became rich in content. We even sang concert songs while marching to or from work.

*Today is not the time to laugh*
*So I've just been told;*
*But I do just the opposite.*
*I don't give a damn;*
*I won't transform the world*
*Because it's not worthy.*

A special hit was the song I created right after my arrival in Skarżysko, "In the Skarżysko Lager":

*In a quiet, thick forest*
*Stands the Lager wired round.*
*I tell you, people here are treated like garbage;*
*The Lager does not*
*Differentiate between rich and poor.*
*For many months I've been suffering here*
*But from the present noise one can become deaf.*
*The mass murders break one's heart;*
*No words are adequate to express my pain.*
*How bitter it is in Skarżysko Lager.*
*This Skarżysko Lager, Good God,*
*The mere thought of it*
*Causes my hands and feet to tremble.*
*Would that I had never known this place.*

Every evening the program ended with this song, sung by the whole crowd, like a hymn. Thanks to the artistic and literary people who came to us from Majdanek, we had a new program every week. Every evening after work I would sit down with my new friend Mordechai to write Yiddish or Polish poetry and sketches or satires about Lager life.

The concerts were a balm for the physically and spiritually broken prisoners. I recall one Sunday morning when Mordechai and I were finishing a new sketch for that evening and having trouble with a closing line. The barrack was empty, we thought, because the night shift workers had not yet returned from work. We suddenly heard a quiet voice from a corner. We turned to see a young man, around twenty years of age, who looked half-dead. He could barely raise his head as he looked at us through half-shut eyes. He called my name and gave me a closing line for the song. Then he asked if he would be able to attend the concert that evening. He died that day.

The death rate in Skarżysko was so high that if the war continued for much longer, the Nazis wouldn't need to shoot anyone – we all would die of hunger anyhow. It was a miracle that some workers still managed to smuggle in food acquired through illegal trading with the gentile workers. They were both risking their lives because the Nazis would severely punish, or even put to death, anyone who attempted to improve our lot.

Besides my struggle to survive yet another day of hard physical work, I continued to worry about my father and three sisters, who had been transported to Poniatowa in December 1942. I tried once again to make use of my friendly connection with Gastomski. Initially he refused my request, worried that he'd be caught with the letters during the count. But seeing my desperation, he agreed to go at the end of June. When he returned after a few days, he gave me a signal to meet in the latrine; our meetings had to proceed with the greatest caution as we had to guard ourselves against not only the Germans but also Antek. Both of us were risking our lives. Gastomski told me how he had journeyed to Poniatowa and how the whole region was surrounded by thousands of Nazis, making it dangerous to be out in the street.

Still, he had succeeded in reaching the town and finding the workshop in the Lager. To this day I don't know how he got in, since there was a military guard at the gate – he never told me the particulars of this dangerous mission – but I thanked God that Gastomski's trip had come to a safe and successful conclusion.

I carefully hid the pack of letters for the Staszówer prisoners and we both returned to the factory. Out of fear, we did not exchange even one word that day. When, after work, we were lined up in rows of five to return to the Lager I had a feeling that something was going to happen and silently prayed to pass the daily inspection at the gate. The inspection passed without problems, with the guard just asking if I had taken anything from the factory. But after the inspection, as we started to disperse, I heard my name being called in Polish.

A Ukrainian *Werkschutz* came up to me with his rifle on his shoulder and ordered me to follow him. I felt that this was the end for me. Should he discover the letters and money that I was carrying, he could take them away and shoot me on the spot. He led me close to the barbed wire, not far from the watchtower, and said, "I know that you get letters and money from outside. Hand them to me and nothing will happen to you." I tried to get out of this predicament by saying that it was not true. He beat me with his gun, striking me down. At that moment, a miracle happened: a group of curious men and women gathered round and the *Werkschutz* turned around to chase away the observers. I quickly took the bundle of letters out of my shirt, shoved them aside and slowly got up. The guard didn't find anything on me. Friends later found the package of letters intact and helped me distribute them among the Staszówer *landsleit*, or landsmen. I was overjoyed that the letters had been rescued and anxious to read my father's words.

*We are working twelve hours a day under heavy military watch. The food here is much worse than in Staszów and there's no possibility of getting anything else, even for money. But the worst thing is that there is no medical help for the sick. My dear David, I must tell you further that your sister Tova Leah died ten days ago after suffering from tuberculosis. I take solace in the fact that maybe it's better to die in bed instead of by a bullet and this is what I tell the children to comfort them. We live here for the moment and don't know what the morrow will bring. No doubt you know what happened during the Staszówer resettlement in November. The only ones from our family who were able to save themselves were my sister's children, your cousins, the Parizers. They all left for Warsaw before the resettlement. May God grant that they be spared our fate. My dear son, thanks to your messenger I know how you are faring there in Skarżysko. Guard your health after your last illness so that if anything happens to us at least you will remain alive. I end with warm regards and kisses from Faigele and Rokhelle. Your father, Itche.*

I couldn't fall asleep that night as I thought about my sister Tova Leah, who had been only twenty-five. Tears choked me, but I tried to control myself so as not to wake up my neighbours with my crying.

~

Another typhus epidemic began to spread among the new arrivals from Majdanek and hundreds of sick men and women died or were taken from Barrack 7. The ranks of those capable of working shrank each day. My friend Natek Neugarten became ill and barely made it through the twelve-hour work shift to return to the barrack. I carried him over to the sick barrack where another friend diagnosed him with typhus. Now we found ourselves in a dilemma: should he remain in the Lager and not go to work? He had no strength, so how would he be able to work? Still, we decided that it would be best if Natek went to work, sick as he was, instead of risking going to Barrack 7.

For ten days I carried him on my shoulders from our barrack to the factory and back, thus helping him avoid selection. I was able to convince the Polish *Meister*, or foreman, Biernatski, to allow Natek to just sit and not work for the duration of his sickness, but this had to be in strict secrecy, and I also had to give Antek a cash bribe. These were ten days of great sacrifice until his health improved.

The typhus epidemic eventually eased somewhat but not the hunger. Even so, our will to live, even in such inhumane conditions, was so strong that it did not occur to any of us to commit suicide. Just the opposite – the more we endured, the stronger our will to live became. This was our resistance against the degradation.

Our Sunday concerts continued with great success. However, my health began to deteriorate. With the hard labour and the poor food, my feet swelled, forcing me to sleep in my clothes and wooden shoes out of fear that I wouldn't be able to put them on in the morning.

As the summer of 1943 approached, I got the idea of asking *Kommandantin* Markowiczowa to give me more time to devote to the cultural undertakings by freeing me from my shell-making work. She recommended me for a place in the *Ordnungsdienst*, where I would be responsible for getting a group of thirty-five men and women to work on time. It was hard for me to accept this job because I felt that I would be helping the Nazis, and it was a difficult role to take on. However, the alternative was to remain in the artillery factory, which was harmful to my health.

In the end, I decided to take the new job. The management for this force was in Jewish hands, though the SS still had their Ukrainian helpers who had the upper hand. This meant there were opportunities for Jews to help one another, though some used their new authority brutally. When I started my job, I tried to ease the spirit of the group I was in charge of. They were the ones who worked under the most unhealthy and difficult physical conditions, in the production of the underwater mines made from picric acid. Their work and their yellow, skeletal appearance and torn clothing bothered me. The yellowness was impossible to wash off. My hands and skin took on this yellow colour simply from being in contact with them.

A year earlier, the Jewish workers of *Halle* 13 had gone to work singing and marching as if in the military but now, in the summer months of 1943, they could barely drag themselves to work. Every day, two brutal Nazi *Meister*, Hecht and Zahn, waited for us at the gate. They carefully watched each slave labourer and if, in their opinion, anyone appeared incapable of fulfilling the demands of the twelve-hour workday, the name of that person was written down. What this meant was not a secret; when the selections took place, those whose names had been recorded were the first to be sent to their death. For this reason, every man and woman tried not to fall behind in the production line.

Alter, my friend from my hometown who came to Werk C with the group from Sandomierz, was assigned to *Halle* 53, where I had worked, making artillery shells. After only a few weeks, he got sick with tuberculosis. Fortunately, the Germans didn't order those with this illness to Barrack 7. When I visited him he told me that the work in the artillery factory was too hard for him and that this was surely the reason for his illness. He asked me to intervene with the camp elders to see if he could be freed from the heavy work.

Recalling what had happened to my sister, who had died of tuberculosis in Poniatowa, I agreed to intervene to save my friend. I convinced the *Kommandantin* and Biernatski that Alter could get better if he no longer had to work in *Halle* 53. I was delighted when, despite the primitive medical help, Alter came out relatively healthy and got a job in the local administration. He was so happy that he, too, could finally go every other Sunday to Werk A to have a warm bath. We all thought it was a blessing to go there and meet friends and acquaintances who, because of the lighter working conditions, looked relatively better than us, though the two camps were not that far from each other.

The Germans and the Ukrainian guards coordinated their brutal management of all three camps in Skarżysko, but the death rate in Werk C was highest. The ranks of those gathered for the march to work became more and more sparse. Much of the audience for the Sunday night concerts was gone, and the Sunday evening performances took place less regularly.

Because of the high death rate we felt sure that the Nazis would soon put an end to Skarżysko. Sometimes, we envied the dead, who were through with it all; at other times we hoped that, by some miracle, we'd survive the war. After work, we waited impatiently to return to our barrack to get our piece of bread or bit of soup and share the latest news about the war. We took courage from the false hope that the German armies would soon be defeated.

~

In July 1943, I convinced my friend Gastomski to go once again to Poniatowa. With great difficulty, he managed to make connections with the Lager there. He brought back a few letters but no money. My father wrote that rumours were circulating that the Germans would soon liquidate the tailoring shops, and there was even talk about a "resettlement." The only question was, where to? I wouldn't hear until much later that, in early autumn 1943, Poniatowa had become a sub-camp of the nearby Majdanek death camp.

On November 8, 1943, Gastomski arrived in Poniatowa for the last time. I was shocked by the news that he brought back: he had no letters from our dear families. I had the feeling that the worst had happened. Then he told me that, according to the reports of Polish witnesses, hundreds of heavily armed SS and Ukrainians had surrounded the Lager on November 3. They chased everyone – men, women and children alike – out of the barracks and forced them to dig their own grave. After they were forced to undress, they were shot. The shooting lasted over an hour. Shrieks and cries were heard through loudspeakers, together with classical music. This was later called the Harvest Festival.

I couldn't bear this news, and I burst out crying. When I passed the news on to my Staszówer neighbours in my barrack, we said the Kaddish prayer together with tears in our eyes. We asked each other how much longer it would be before the murderers killed us, too.

# Hanka

We soon learned from the Lager administrators that a new transport was to arrive with fresh victims for Werk C. Every time a new group arrived, we hoped that maybe the handling of the prisoners would improve because, after all, there was a shortage of workers. On November 16, 1943, a transport of 2,500 men and women arrived from slave labour in Płaszów, near Krakow.

A few weeks later, I saw my friend Alter. I was happy that his health had significantly improved. He was grateful that I had used my influence with *Kommandantin* Markowiczowa, and asked me to take him to her so that he could thank her with a small gift. That evening after work we both went to the White House. When I timidly knocked at the *Kommandantin*'s door and explained to her the reason for our visit, she refused to accept the gift and instead invited me into the room, saying that she wanted me to meet her guests, who were staying with her.

Three women were seated at the table. They had just arrived on the latest transport from Płaszów and were celebrating the birthday of the youngest. One of the women, Tashke, was a friend of Fela's from before the war. Tashke had lived in Tarnów with her husband and child. During the deportation from Tarnów, it was her fate to go to the right instead of to the left with her husband and child, who were sent to their death.

The other women, Esther and her niece, Hanka, had gone through a similar experience in Tarnów. They reported that during the first deportation they had succeeded in hiding in a bakery, in a large oven, together with four more people from their family. After two days they came out, barely alive. But during the second deportation they stood in the large market with thousands of others during the selection. Esther and her niece were told to go to the right while Esther's two children, ages twelve and fourteen, who by chance were standing with Hanka's mother, Yochevet, were sent to the left.

In the great confusion, no one knew that going to the left was a death sentence. After the thousands of exhausted men, women and children were sent in the packed cattle cars to Treblinka, the Nazis sent the rest to Płaszów. Many branches of Hanka and Esther's family were among those sent to Treblinka, brutally ending several hundred years of Jewish life in Tarnów.

I was deeply moved when they spoke of how they were separated from their family. From the moment that Esther and her sister's daughter, Hanka, were sent away together to Werk C, they stuck together like a mother and child. This made such an impression on me that I visited my new friends daily and we spent every free minute together after work.

Some of the new arrivals were assigned to a relatively easy job in *Halle* 12, the Schmitz factory, where anti-tank bullets and detonators were assembled. Others were sent to Werk A, where the working conditions were relatively easier. When Hanka informed me that her two cousins were in Werk A, I was able to arrange for them to work for the Lager administration.

~

The last months of 1943 were very hard for us to bear. It was a difficult winter, and production in the munitions factory was increased because of the defeats of the German armies on the eastern front. At the same time, the *Werkschutz* tightened the watch on the exits from the factory for the outside gentile workers and especially for the Jewish slave labourers at the entrance to the camp. Thus the contact with the gentile workers was cut off, making our previous trades impossible.

It was also harder to take out parts of guns and ammunition for the Polish anti-Nazi movement. When the Germans found a piece of leather that two Jews, a father and a son, had brought into the Lager to repair their torn shoes, they were immediately arrested. We understood that the Nazis would use this incident to punish these two prisoners and scare the rest of us, who had risked smuggling in essentials to ease our lives.

Soon after, the Germans announced that on Sunday at 10:00 a.m., all men and women had to be at the roll-call place to witness a prepared spectacle. There was to be a public execution. When everyone was brought from the barracks to the assembly point, two gallows had already been set up. The two victims, father and son, were standing nearby, guarded by *Werkschutz* who were responsible for carrying out the hanging. But first the SS-*Obersturmführer* gave a fiery speech, warning against the enemies of the Third Reich.

The German and Ukrainian guards forced us not to lower our eyes but to look straight ahead as they hanged first the son and then the father. The double murder was not enough to satisfy them – they wanted to make sure that the condemned father would see his son hanged. We stood dumbstruck, witnessing the terrible scene; too fearful to make a sound, we swallowed our tears. When we returned to our barracks after this appalling spectacle, we said Kaddish.

In spite of this tragedy, the Sunday evening performance took place at the same time as usual. We had to do this to avoid falling into a state of depression because that was the aim of the Nazis: to break us physically and morally before totally doing away with us.

That evening was a cold one and the whole Lager was covered with a layer of fresh snow. When I left the concert with Hanka, the moon was bright, as though to tease us. Nature was so beautiful, but not for the suffering. As we made our way together between the barracks we saw something in the distance – a body that could hardly move. When we got closer we saw that this was a barely alive *Muselmann*. He looked like an old man, but was no more than twenty. He didn't answer our question of what he was doing there, but we saw that from beneath the snow he had pulled out a skeleton and was trying to suck the marrow from the dried-up bones. The two of us stood there, without uttering a word. Finally, after managing to tear the desperate man from the skeleton, we took him to his barrack. I didn't sleep all night, thinking about what hunger can lead to. Even so, as I mentioned, I don't recall one case of suicide. We had to believe that we would outlive the greatest enemy of all mankind. Somewhere in us, there remained a spark of hope that we could live to see the day of victory over Nazism.

~

Witnessing the execution of the father and son had convinced Hanka and her aunt Esther to try to get transferred to Werk A. The elder of the Lager was Herr Albirt, who had several aides around him, including the second-in-command of the Jewish *Ordnungsdienst*, Josef K. His secretary was my friend Hanka's cousin, Fela.

Although the new camp commander in Werk A, Paul Kuehnemann, roamed around with a large dog and always carried a riding whip in his hand, which he used quite often, working conditions were better and those who worked there could go to the bathhouse at least once a week. One Sunday, when we came from Werk C to bathe, Hanka and Esther met their cousin Fela and asked her to intervene with the Jewish elder to allow the two of them to be transferred to Werk A. Fela promised to do all she could so that they could be together.

In March 1944, thanks to Fela's intervention, they were both transferred to Werk A. I was left lonely because of the move. Hanka and Esther seemed to feel the same way because a few weeks later I was called to the office, where I was told that an order had arrived to transfer me to Werk A. My joy was indescribable. After a year and a half in the hell of Werk C, I was now to be with my close friends and perhaps have better living conditions. I was sorry to leave my friends in the munitions plant, after working, starving and suffering with them for so long. Still, when I was taken to the other Lager, Hanka and Esther were delighted, as was I. I thanked them and their cousin Fela for getting me out of Werk C.

I immediately joined the existing drama group, which also carried out weekly concerts in Polish and Yiddish, outdoors if the weather permitted. I brought along my whole repertoire from Werk C and very soon all were singing along to the songs.

The treatment was in fact much the same as in Werk C, and the food rations were insufficient, as always. However, contact with the Polish workers was easier, and we could smuggle in food.

In the spring of 1944, we heard news that the Germans were being defeated on all fronts, which made us feel much better. Our morale further improved when we heard that the Soviet army had begun a counter-offensive and the Germans were retreating in great confusion.

From our Polish co-workers in the munitions factories we learned that *Reichsführer-SS* Himmler had ordered the liquidation of three death camps in eastern Poland – Sobibor, Belzec and Treblinka – so as not to leave any trace of Nazi terror. We also learned from witnesses in Werk C that near the Lager, where the Nazis had killed those who were sick with typhus, hundreds of Poles suspected of anti-Nazi activities were now being brought for execution. Among the victims there were even some priests. To destroy the evidence, the victims were burned; people could smell the smoke from their burning bodies.

We feared that Himmler's order might mean our camp's liquidation as well. It did not take long: at the end of June 1944 we learned that the Germans had decided to evacuate the three HASAG munitions factories and take the Jewish slave labourers to Germany. None of us believed that thousands of Jews would be taken alive to Germany. We doubted they would make an exception for us and suspected they would treat us in the same way as they had the prisoners of Sobibor, Belzec and Treblinka.

The SS ordered everyone to gather on August 1, 1944, at the roll-call place, from where we were to march to the train. I later heard the following story about *Kommandantin* Markowiczowa: She had decided this time not to carry out the Nazis orders. Since taking over the command of Werk C, she had befriended some Ukrainian *Werkschutz* who visited her often in the White House. When she found out that the Nazis wanted to evacuate, the Ukrainian *Werkschutz* told her that they would help her and her whole family escape.

Around 2:00 a.m. on July 31, when everyone was asleep, the barbed wire was cut and Fela Markowiczowa and her whole family left, together with the members of the administration and a few friends and acquaintances – a total of fifty people. No sooner had they gone deeper into the forest than the Ukrainians opened fire on the unarmed group. Everyone perished except for Fela's mother, Frau Gutman, who lay beneath the bodies of her children and grandchildren. She was the only surviving witness of this barbaric mass murder. She managed to reach the hut of a Polish peasant, where she lived until the end of the war.

The next morning the Germans brought everyone to the railway station in Skarżysko, where armed SS soldiers and transport trains were already waiting for us. When the Nazis began to shove us into the trains, we were sure that we were being taken to our death. *Lagerführer* Kuehnemann used his leather riding whip to hurry people on board. I got my share from him before I managed to get into the same wagon as Hanka, her aunt Esther and her cousin Fela.

After we were packed into the trains, the Nazis locked the wagons to ensure no one would escape. It was so crowded that it was almost impossible to breathe. A bit of sunshine and air came in through a small window grate. When the train finally began to move, we still did not know where we were being taken. No one panicked, but we were all prepared for the worst.

After travelling for several hours, the train came to a stop in Częstochowa, Poland, where about two hundred men and women were taken off to work at the munitions factory there. Only then did the Germans give us bread and water. We continued to travel all night until we reached Leipzig, in eastern Germany, at dawn.

When the train came to a stop and the doors of the wagons finally opened, my heart started to beat faster. The Germans ordered all the women to leave while the men remained in place. When I said goodbye to Hanka, I was frightened that we were saying goodbye forever. Hanka told me that if, in spite of everything, we survived the war, we should meet in her hometown of Tarnów. She gave me her address, which engraved itself in my memory.

# Buchenwald

After the SS locked the wagon doors, the train remained standing for some time, allowing us to observe through the small window the Germans leading the women away in rows of five. It was only at noon that the train started to move again. I was so wrapped up in thoughts about the outcome of the journey that I completely forgot it had been twenty-four hours since I had last had a piece of bread.

The train slowly continued on its way for a few more hours until it came to a stop in the historic city of Weimar. It struck me that not far from here was the infamous concentration camp of Buchenwald, which I had heard about because it had been constructed in 1937. Were we really being taken there? The thought of the horrors I might face there filled me with fear.

The locked doors were finally opened and I, along with a hungry, tired and frightened mass, got down from the wagons. We saw a gigantic Lager with hundreds of barracks and houses surrounded by barbed wire and a row of watchtowers. To the right of the main entrance stood a crematorium with a very high chimney; a thin white cloud of smoke rose up from it. I wondered if this was how the crematoria in Auschwitz looked.

The SS ordered us to line up in rows of five and, after counting us, marched us through the main gate where, engraved in iron, was the sign *Jedem das Seine* ("To each his own"); *Recht oder Unrecht – mein*

*Vaterland* ("Right or wrong – my country") was written on a gate-house nearby.

Everything we had was taken away from us, including the clothes we were wearing. We were then sent to a shower room, where a group of barbers shaved our entire bodies and, for hygienic reasons I assume, spread a chemical substance on us that burned our skin. We still didn't believe that the Nazis would let us live if there were thousands of *Häftlinge*, prisoners, already there. It was only when water, not gas, started flowing from the overhead taps that we breathed freely and thought that our lives would enter a new chapter. Upon exiting the bath we each received a long, striped uniform consisting of a pair of pants, a jacket and a pair of shoes. For the first time since our journey from Skarżysko I let out a hearty laugh – our appearance was comical. A tall man, for instance, received a pair of pants that reached only to his knees while a short person got a jacket or coat big enough for two. Naturally, people exchanged clothes.

We were next sent into a large hall for registration where we each got a number that would be our "passport" from that moment forth. Sewn onto each uniform was the new identity replacing each prisoner's name; mine was 68577. Completing all the formalities took several hours. Then, members of the administration took over. Two Yiddish-speaking *Häftlinge*, Gustav from Lemberg and Elek from Tarnów, introduced themselves. They had come on behalf of the Jewish political prisoners to explain to us the structure in Buchenwald and tell us that we need not be afraid.

They first wanted to know about our experiences in Skarżysko, about the working conditions and especially about the treatment by the kapos, supervisors. We listened with great interest but little trust. We didn't believe that we could trust these strangers with our tragic experiences of the years in the Skarżysko hell. Gradually, however, we newcomers began to disclose what was in our hearts, telling the two men our personal stories of life in Skarżysko, about the difficult work conditions, the brutal treatment and about certain members of the Jewish leadership.

Gustav and Elek listened to the complaints and promised to visit us the following day to record the names of the ones responsible, who were now among us. Finally we were taken to a small Lager, the "Little Camp," where there were barracks and tents. The *Zeltlager*, tent camp, served as an intermediate point from which the Nazis would take the new arrivals to the so-called Buchenwald *Aussenkommandos*, satellite camps.

It was only now that we got a portion of bread and marmalade and a cup of coffee and could lie down to rest for the first time since leaving Skarżysko. While talking to some of the veterans, we were told that the inner administration had been in the hands of SS-*Obersturmbannführer* Karl-Otto Koch from 1937 until 1941. This criminal and his helpers had killed thousands of prisoners. The SS, which had its quarters in the main building at the entrance to the camp, had given anyone in charge free reign to deal harshly with prisoners, even for the most minor fault. For their "good deeds" they were rewarded with a double portion of food. We were also told that the SS, together with the kapos, had a quota of dead to bring back each day from work outside the camp. The kapos brought back the dead to ensure that the number of prisoners corresponded morning and evening. If the count didn't match, the prisoners would stand for many hours, summer and winter, until the SS *Lagerführer* terminated the roll call. It was only then that they could each return to their barrack to get their daily portion of bread.

Prisoners worked in the stone quarry, which was several kilometres from the Lager, as well as in the Deutsche-Ausrüstungs-Werke, German Equipment Works, which was operated by the SS, in camp workshops and in an adjacent munitions plant. These sites were also surrounded by electrified barbed wire. The SS who guarded the workers would mockingly order certain inmates to run to the barbed wire. The victims' choice was to die from a German bullet or be electrocuted. The kapos, on the other hand, would choke their victims or beat them to death.

German SS doctors in Buchenwald had a special block where they conducted all kinds of medical experiments on specially selected prisoners, experiments that ended in their death. There was also a block, separate from the rest of the Lager, for women whose job it was to sexually satisfy the SS administration as a reward for their hard work for the good of the Third Reich. The Nazis constantly changed the women, who came from various concentration camps; since they were never in contact with the interned men, we didn't know if Jewish women were there. Only one woman had contact with the prisoners – Ilse Koch, the wife of the former commandant of Buchenwald, Karl-Otto Koch, and her name alone caused a shudder. Hundreds of people had perished by her hand. Her husband was transferred to Majdanek in 1941 and later paid for his evil actions with his life in 1945. After the war, Ilse was put in prison, where she committed suicide in 1967.

From further talks with the prisoners who had been in the camp a long time, known as the "veterans," we learned that after the removal of Koch, a new administrator, Hermann Pister, had come in 1942. At the same time, Erich Reschke, a German communist arrested for his beliefs in 1933 and imprisoned in Buchenwald since 1938, became the camp elder. This new leadership organized an anti-Nazi underground committee. In contrast to the earlier years, the non-Jewish prisoners treated the Jews with respect. When we arrived in Buchenwald, the conditions and the rations were much better than in previous years and much better than in Skarżysko.

On our second day, Gustav and Elek visited us again. They wanted to know the names of those in charge of the three Skarżysko camps who had used their authority inhumanely. When they declared that the guilty ones would pay for their conduct, nobody believed them. But two days later, six of these people mysteriously vanished from our group, and nothing more was heard about them.

We remained in the *Zeltlager* for a week or so until most of our group of several hundred was ordered to a different Lager to work in the munitions factory in the Buchenwald *Aussenkommando* in the city of Schlieben. Prior to our arrival, the communist anti-Nazi group, some of whom were Jews, had successfully persuaded the SS to keep the children and youth in Buchenwald by telling them the children would be taught "German discipline." They also intervened in the work assignments so that Mordechai Strigler and I could stay in camp and teach the Jewish children. I was amazed to be granted the privilege of remaining and doing this type of work in such dire circumstances. Once again, I had to say goodbye to friends and acquaintances with whom I had gone through so much.

The same day that the group was transported to Schlieben, those remaining from our group were taken to Block 23, in the centre of the larger Lager, not far from the place where thousands of internees gathered every day for the roll calls, which lasted for several hours. An orchestra played at the beginning and end of the roll call, and the SS made sure that every group marched to the beat of the music.

Jewish veterans from various European countries lived in our block, many of whom belonged to the various active anti-Nazi movements. These blocks were not like the wooden barracks in Skarżysko. For example, Block 23 was a one-storey building with a dining hall, a dormitory with military beds and a clean washroom. The conditions were significantly better; most importantly, the building was free of lice. Every block had a radio loudspeaker, and every evening after work the military radio broadcast the news from the war front, as well as various orders for the internees.

Each day, I was able to speak with Jews and non-Jews from various countries. In spite of the language differences, one goal united us: to survive. At some point after our arrival, the Nazis brought in a transport from Denmark consisting of members of the Danish police force who had refused to collaborate with the Nazi regime. Engraved in my memory is a conversation I had with a few of them, who told me that they had rescued thousands in the Jewish population by transporting them to Sweden.

Not far from our block was a diplomatic block to which we had no access because it was heavily guarded. Political leaders from various countries were held there, including the Jewish former prime minister of France, Léon Blum. He was interned together with other French political activists. Ernst Thälmann, leader of the pre-war communist party in Germany, was also kept there, in solitary confinement. Rudolf Breitscheid of the German Social Democratic Party was held there as well.

When we arrived at Buchenwald, some people managed to sneak in a few children. The lawyer Zacharias Zweig and his three-year-old son, Jerzy, also called Juschu, had come in with us. Zacharias, his wife, Helena, their seven-year-old daughter, Sylwia, and Juschu had arrived in Skarżysko in November 1943 from Płaszów. Helena Zweig and her daughter remained with the women's transport in Leipzig, and Zacharias Zweig somehow managed to bring Juschu into the Lager in a backpack. It is truly amazing that the child didn't cry at all during our trip in the packed wagons, especially at the entrance of the camp. But news about the child soon became known. A kapo, a German communist named Willi Bleicher, approached Zweig, offering to take the child to his comfortable living quarters where he could live undisturbed and his father could visit him. Zweig had no other choice and let him take Jerzy. Zweig was assigned, together with the small group from Skarżysko, to our block and would tell us every day how the child was faring.

On August 15, I was assigned to work three days a week in a construction command, near the Gustloff Werke munitions factory where thousands were manufacturing V-1 and V-2 weaponry; in September I was assigned to a drainage command. The other three days, my friend Mordechai and I were busy teaching approximately sixty Jewish children from different countries. Though we had no school texts, we managed to give them a grounding in Jewish history, educate them about the holidays, and teach them songs. The lessons took place in secret in our dormitory. Once, an SS patrol happened to come by our block. The children quickly dispersed through the windows, so we all fortunately escaped serious consequences.

One day in August I was placed with a group of bricklayers to freshen up the house of the SS-*Hauptsturmführer*, not far from the Lager gate. The house entrance was heavily guarded by two armed SS men with large dogs. When we arrived for work, we were received by the *Hauptsturmführer*'s wife. We worked there the whole day until five o'clock in the evening. She gave each of us a portion of bread with margarine and a cup of coffee and watched us from a distance, as though we had come from another planet.

Finally, she decided to start a conversation with me. I happened to be the youngest in the group, and maybe this was why she spoke to me. When she realized that I understood German, she began to ask me where I was born, my nationality, how long I had been in Buchenwald and whom I had killed, since she believed only murderers were imprisoned in Buchenwald. It was very hard to convince her that my only crime was being a Jew. She also did not believe that I was the only survivor from my whole family. Afterwards, I regretted telling her, worrying there might be consequences, but I was lucky, and the incident passed.

Due to my connections to various people, I gained access to the office near the camp's main entrance. I wanted to get news about Hanka and her aunt because I had no idea what had happened to them since our separation. Through the help of one of the office employees, I entered the section where records were kept of not only all the prisoners in the Lager but also those in the satellite camps. I knew that the labour camp in Leipzig was under the jurisdiction of Buchenwald, and I prayed to find their names among the living so that I could write to them. The German employee allowed me to search the books until I came across the Lager in Leipzig and found the list of its new arrivals. I learned that the camp produced ammunition and that a few women had been sent to Ravensbrück, among them Helena Zweig and her young daughter, as well as Hanka's cousin Fela. I later found out that Helena Zweig and her daughter were murdered in September 1944. I wrote down the prisoner numbers of the women so that I could write to them, but I wondered how I could dispatch a letter from Buchenwald and whether it would reach its destination. I sought an answer for a few days.

Though there were brutal members of the SS who, without any questions or protests, carried out sadistic acts, there were those few who, in their hearts, opposed the Nazi regime. So it was that through the anti-Nazi movement I met such a German, an SS officer, who came into the Lager from time to time. To my great surprise he promised me that he would send the letter, but he told me to write it in German and to be very careful with the contents, since the letters were heavily censored.

I immediately wrote a letter to Hanka and gave it to the German, who even paid for the postage stamp himself. I truthfully did not believe that it would arrive at its destination, so I wrote another letter a few weeks later and once again gave it to my German. I waited a long time for a reply, but unfortunately none came.

~

*December 3, 1944*

*Dearest Maman and Aunt!*

*I have anxiously been waiting for a letter from you for so long. I have written perhaps 5 times, but until now, not a word. It's possible that you didn't receive my letters. I beg you, dearest, to send me a letter. I am doing quite well. I frequently receive letters from my brother; he writes that he is doing very well. He longs for Hanka ... He has met Schomek and Ivo Gross, [Leiner] and others. He advised and helped them a lot before they left. And now to me: I am healthy, content with everything; but I miss you. How are Aunt, Tosia, and all our friends? I am sure that they are all healthy. Very best wishes for your birthday (although it's already past). Give my greetings to all our friends. Many kisses to you and Aunt. Your David.*

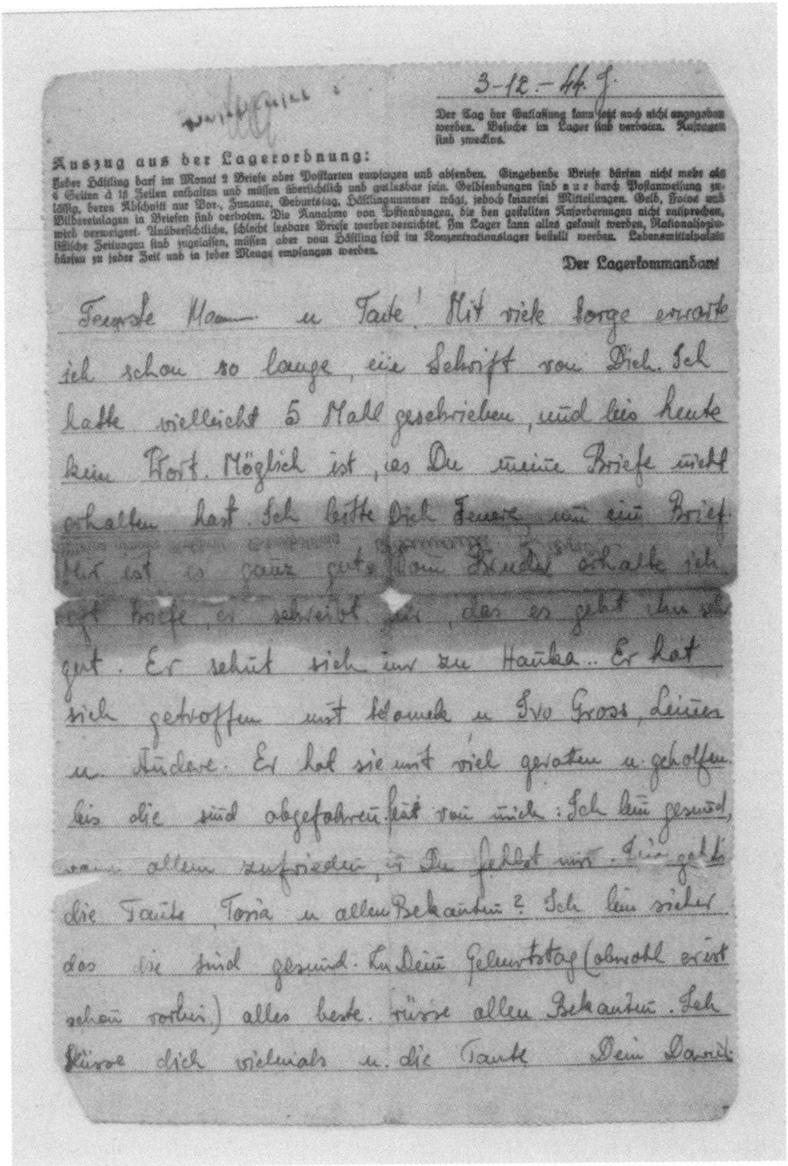

[Translation of typewritten German: The release date cannot yet be given. Visits to the camp are not permitted. Requests are futile. Excerpt from the camp rules: Each inmate may receive and send 2 letters or postcards per month. Incoming letters may be no longer than 4 pages of 15 lines each and must be clear and legible. Money may be sent only by postal money order with only the given name, surname, date of birth, and number of the prisoner but no messages. Money, photos, or pictures in letters are not permitted. Mail items that do not conform to the requirements will not be accepted. Unclear or difficult-to-read letters will be destroyed. Everything is available for purchase in the camp. National socialist newspapers are allowed but must be ordered by the concentration camp inmate him- or herself. Food parcels may be received at any time and in any quantity.]

[The camp commandant.]

*January 13, 1945*

*Dearest Maman and Aunt!*

*I have already written to you many times and I am still without a reply. I also wrote to you last week. Do you really have no opportunity to write? I will not be at peace until I have news of you. With me, everything is fine. I am healthy, content with everything. My only wish is a letter from you. How are you? Are you healthy? Two months ago I met my "rival"; he is together with his brother Ivo. I gave the two of them a lot of advice. Greetings and kisses to all our friends: Tosia, Fela, Esther, Tamara and others. Waiting impatiently for an answer, your David.*

⁓

After the war, I learned that a man in Schlieben had written to his wife in Leipzig that David Neiman remained in Buchenwald and had become a teacher of Jewish souls. The woman understood that Jewish souls were only to be found in heaven and, thinking I was dead, was afraid to convey the news to Hanka. Hanka learned the truth when she eventually received my two letters, but she was unable to find some means to write back to me.

13T 451

Der Tag der Entlassung kann jetzt noch nicht angegeben werden. Besuche im Lager sind verboten. Anfragen sind zwecklos.

**Auszug aus der Lagerordnung:**

Jeder Häftling darf im Monat 2 Briefe oder Postkarten empfangen und absenden. Eingehende Briefe dürfen nicht mehr als 4 Seiten à 15 Zeilen enthalten und müssen übersichtlich und gut lesbar sein. Geldsendungen sind nur durch Postanweisung zulässig, bezw. deren Abschnitt nur Vor-, Zunamen, Geburtstag, Häftlingsnummer trägt, jedoch keinerlei Mitteilungen. Geld, Fotos und Bildereinlagen in Briefen sind verboten. Die Annahme von Postsendungen, die den gestellten Anforderungen nicht entsprechen, wird verweigert. Unübersichtliche, schlecht lesbare Briefe werde vernichtet. Im Lager kann alles gekauft werden, Nationalsozialistische Zeitungen sind zugelassen, müssen aber vom Häftling selbst im Konzentrationslager bestellt werden. Lebensmittelpakete dürfen zu jeder Zeit und in jeder Menge empfangen werden.

Der Lagerkommandant

Liebste Mammiün u. Tauk!
Schon vielmals hab' ich an Dich geschrieben
und bis jetzt bin ich ohne Antwort.
Auch die vergangene Woche habe ich
an Dich geschrieben. Hast du wirklich
keine Möglichkeit? Ich habe keine
Ruh bis ich von Dir keine Nachricht
bekomme. Bei mir alles in Ordnung. Ich bin
gesund von allem zufrieden. Mein
ist nur ein Brief von Euch. Wie geht's Euch?
Seid ihr gesund? Ich habe vor 2 Monaten mein
"Rival" getroffen, er war zusammen mit sein
Brüder Wo. Ich hab die Beiden viel
geraten kurze u. Kuss allen Bekannten: Tonia,
Fila, Erika, Tamara u. andere. Dein
mit Ungeduld wartender, auf Antwort.
685 F.
Daniel

On August 24, 1944, when I went with my group to work near the munitions factory in Gustloff Werke, all of us were excited because of the good news from the front. We heard that Soviet troops were defeating the Germans in the Polish cities near the Soviet border. We also heard that the Western armies had opened a second front and that the American air force was bombing German cities. Nature also played its part in improving our mood; the sun was shining and the sky was clear blue, free of clouds. We had the feeling that something out of the ordinary would happen very soon.

When the orchestra began to play the march during roll call, we actually felt like singing along. The talk among the prisoners that day was about the American Second Front at Normandy and about whether the democratic forces of the world would be able to defeat the German giant. Our discussion lasted until noon, when we sat down to rest for half an hour. Suddenly, we heard the roar of airplanes. We could not have imagined that these were not the German planes that regularly patrolled the skies – we didn't even dream that Allied planes could reach all the way here. But suddenly a few American planes swept down, flying so low that we recognized their markings and even saw the faces of the pilots. Their aim was perfect. With great accuracy, they bombed the whole area of the factory, and we heard the explosions.

During the bombing, hundreds of prisoners and SS perished, their torn bodies strewn over the whole area of the destroyed factory. I was wounded in my left leg and lay on the ground until all the wounded were taken away to the sick quarters. The Allied pilots had struck with amazing accuracy – the Gustloff Werke was very close to the Lager and not one bomb fell there during the whole attack. This raises the question: why didn't the Allied forces bomb the railway lines leading to Auschwitz, Treblinka and others in 1942 and 1943, which would have perhaps reduced the number of deaths?

The Nazis took advantage of these circumstances. Under the pretext that two of the political prisoners – Ernst Thälmann and Rudolf

Breitscheid – had been killed during the Allied bombing, the Nazis murdered them. There is still, however, some controversy as to
whether Breitscheid may actually have died in the raid.

When I returned to Block 23 after being hospitalized for two days
for my wounds, I was surrounded by a lot of confusion. Because of
the destroyed munitions factory, thousands remained in the camp
without being assigned to any other work. Chaos also prevailed in all
sections of the administration. The SS command seemed to be con-
fused by the air attack.

When news spread about the death of Ernst Thälmann, the anti-
Nazi committee decided to conduct a memorial. About one month
later, in the strictest secrecy, delegates from various national groups
of internees were chosen to attend. The Jewish group also sent representatives, and I was one of the members delegated to participate
in the memorial. In the cellar of the canteen building a group of veterans gathered, together with a few *Lagerschutz*, camp guards, who
checked everyone.

I was overwhelmed when I was asked to sing a mourning song
in German. I was taken into a special room where, to the accom-
paniment of a piano, I sorrowfully sang into a microphone the lul-
laby "Schlaf Kindlein, schlaf" (Sleep my child, sleep). The memorial
was well organized and impressive and ended late in the evening. The
group dispersed cautiously lest, God forbid, we arouse the suspicion
of the SS patrols, who inspected any time they chose.

I heard rumours that the anti-Nazi group had contact with the
outside world by means of an underground secret radio station,
and that the memorial evening for Thälmann had been broadcast
through the airwaves. A few days later, many political activists, especially those who had arranged the memorial, were arrested and sent
to an unknown destination. Someone had betrayed them. It took a
long time until the name of the betrayer became known, but I heard
he got his due at the war's end.

I was afraid of being arrested as well because of my participation in the memorial evening, though I was not present during the actual event. Eventually the fear passed and I continued with my work. Our group went three times a week to clean up the ruins in the bombed munitions factories. The other three days I continued to teach the Jewish children.

~

More transports arrived with Jewish prisoners from various camps that the Nazis had liquidated because of the advancing Soviet army. The largest transports came from Auschwitz and Sachsenhausen. Once, when a transport arrived with Jews from Auschwitz, I was given the job of explaining to them in Polish or Yiddish about the conditions in the Lager and that they need not worry about going into the shower, as they were not gas chambers. Later, from another transport, we found out that a small heroic group had managed to blow up a crematorium in Auschwitz on October 7, 1944, killing some SS guards in the process. Some of these transports remained just a few days before being sent to various labour camps.

The month of September was quite hot, so every spare moment after work was spent outdoors. One Sunday afternoon, the sun was shining and hundreds of prisoners were out walking on the so-called streets, enjoying the good weather and excited to share news about the changing political situation. We had the impression that the gates of Buchenwald would open any minute and we would exit to celebrate the end of the war.

By chance I was walking near the kitchen when I noticed a group of prisoners gathered around a man who was carrying a young child in his arms. The man was the aide of the camp elder and the child was the youngest prisoner, Jerzy Zweig. I stopped to observe young Jerzy and marvel at how well he looked. Suddenly the chauffeur-driven car of the *Hauptsturmführer* parked near the gathered group. The captain was making his weekly inspection round. He went up to the aide and inquired about the child. We knew that nothing good would come out of this episode. When the child's father heard about this, he worried that his son's life was in danger. There was great sadness in our block. No one in our group could help in any way. We just hoped that the child would miraculously survive; after the war, I found out that he did, indeed, survive.

In contrast, one rainy Monday morning, I saw a *Lagerschutz* lead a group of Roma children to the main gate where heavy transport trucks were waiting for them. They marched hand in hand, singing, unaware that the trucks were waiting to take them for what was likely their last journey. After the SS loaded the children onto the transport trucks and drove away, nothing more was heard of them.

# A Spark of Hope

With the arrival of the winter, the Soviet army offensive got stronger and the influx of new internees practically came to a stop. We thought that because of the Soviet victory over the Nazi armies in the east, it would not be long before the Nazi regime totally collapsed. However, German reports over the radio loudspeaker stated the opposite: that the German armies had merely retreated from certain places on the eastern front for strategic reasons. Because of the reduction in fuel supplies caused by Allied bombing, the Germans decided to build a factory for synthetic oil not far from Buchenwald in Berga, Thuringia, on the Elster River.

The SS commandants ordered the camp administration to supply five hundred strong men for the new work in Berga. The anti-Nazi committee, who were in all the head postitions, put together a list of five hundred arrivals from the recently liquidated camps in Poland. The list consisted mainly of Jews and a few French and Czech gentile internees. A committee was also formed that was responsible for the inner administration of the newly formed Lager and had contact with the Jewish political group in Buchenwald. An initial group of seventy prisoners was sent to Berga in mid-November. It was decided that the transport of another five hundred should leave for Berga at the beginning of December 1944.

I was part of the December transport and we arrived at Berga-Elster on December 13, 1944. Before leaving, I took time to say farewell to my friends and acquaintances, especially the group of Jewish children whom I'd had the good fortune to teach. This farewell was very emotional. It was hard for me to part from them, even though I knew that the Jewish section of the anti-Nazi group was working to make conditions easier for them.

We were transported in cattle cars to Berga, a small city not far from Buchenwald. The high hills surrounding the city give the impression that this was a resort, but the Nazis brought us here not for enjoyment but to build an underground factory. Here we no longer had the conveniences of Buchenwald. The large block that had been prepared for our group had served as a military barrack and was surrounded by barbed wire.

The work consisted of twelve-hour days spent breaking stones and rocks in the hills or blowing up the boulders with ammunition. The hygiene facilities were much more primitive than in Buchenwald, though our treatment by the SS was relatively better. We didn't have the Ukrainian collaborators, who used to make trouble for us in Skarżysko, and it was also easier to bring in needed articles from outside through arrangements with German civilians. Some even showed humane feelings and regret for our fate.

It may be that this was just a show of remorse for the crimes committed against us, yet we felt that, compared to a few months earlier, a fresh wind was blowing. During our free time after work, we would gather in small groups and discuss the news we had heard from the Germans about the progress of the war. We also talked about our experiences in the camps. Among us were veterans who had been sent away at the outset of the war, and they did indeed have much to tell.

The well-known French artist Jacob, or Jacques, Markiel was also assigned to our group. He used his free time to draw on the paper that I managed to bring in. He told me about his deportation from Paris to Auschwitz together with thousands of men, women and children who were sent directly to the gas chambers. Miraculously, he had survived.

Though the stone breakers worked day and night, it appeared that the Germans themselves knew that the project of building the plant would never be finished. In the three months since we had arrived at Berga, there was no talk about bringing in any machinery for oil production. Even so, the slave labour continued until April 1945. We knew that the Soviet army had conquered nearly all of Poland and that some concentration camp inmates had probably been freed before the Nazis had a chance to murder them. We also heard that the American army was advancing. We now worried about what the Nazis would do with us. Would they free us here in Germany or carry out Himmler's last order to erase any trace of Nazi barbarity?

The answer came on April 10, 1945, when the SS *Lagerführer* gathered everyone in the roll-call place and announced that the Lager must be liquidated and that we were being evacuated because the Soviet army was advancing and they didn't want us to fall into the hands of the Soviets. He gave us a choice: to travel in cattle cars or to march on foot; however, he didn't tell us where we were going. In spite of this, we unanimously decided that we would go on foot instead of being locked up like cattle in packed trains.

When I set out on the march that day, I felt a spark of hope that this was the final chapter of our enslavement. I had only one wish: to survive the march no matter where it led. We were each given a portion of bread and a cover for sleeping. Under the strict watch of armed SS we left Berga, though not before the *Lagerführer* warned us that we must all stick together and that anyone who fell behind would be shot.

The spring in this part of Germany had come late, but it was a mild day. It had just stopped snowing, the air was pleasant and the days were already getting longer, so we benefited from the sun's warmth on our tired bodies. The first day passed without incident. The stronger prisoners helped the weaker ones so that they wouldn't fall behind and get shot. After we had marched for a few hours, the Germans gave us water and allowed us to rest. When we reached a hamlet that evening, we settled down for the night in a few storehouses. We could barely stretch out our legs because of the crowding, so we passed the night squeezed together.

We continued marching, day in and day out, becoming completely exhausted. Sometimes we were fortunate and the Nazis brought us to a farm that supplied us with water so we could wash. The SS who guarded us got their regular rations from the German population while we made do with the portion of bread that we received every other day. Sometimes, but rarely, the German peasants showed some pity and brought us a warm drink at night.

We dragged ourselves along for 150 kilometres until we reached the Sudetenland. When we went into a storehouse to sleep, the local Czech *Volksdeutsche* brought us bread and warm drinks. We learned from them that we were on the Czech-German border.

The following morning we reached the Czech-German town of Manětín, near Pilsen, the city famous for its beer production. No sooner had we crossed the border into the city than we were greeted warmly, without fear, by hundreds of residents. We didn't understand what was happening – the day before we had been on German territory and treated as though we were criminals, and here we received such a warm greeting.

Later we found out that despite the German occupation of the area back in 1938, the population had fought against the Nazi regime. Young and old now showered us with food, while our SS guards looked on without reacting. Possibly they feared that we might use the opportunity to attack them, or maybe they already knew that the last days of the Nazi regime had arrived. At any rate, we felt that the day of our liberation was fast approaching.

The spontaneous Czech support was a balm, soothing our physical and moral wounds. When the SS appealed to the mayor of Manětín to prepare some storehouses where we could sleep, he refused and instead prepared the large theatre hall for us. Our "protectors" had no choice but to accept the mayor's offer.

At the mayor's order, the Czechs brought bedding, mattresses and even underwear to the theatre. When we marched into the large well-lit theatre hall around noon, everything was ready for us and we slept comfortably for the night. We had no idea how long we would be able to remain there, but we wished that we could stay until the end of the war.

The town residents ignored the presence of the SS guards and brought in various foods, both cooked and raw. I became acquainted with one visitor who, after a long conversation, introduced himself as Dr. Zdenek Baszni, a partisan in a Czech group that operated in the area. He told me that many of his friends had been sent to Buchenwald by the Nazis and that he sympathized with us because we had also come from there. I introduced him to two of my friends, Morits Kalucz, a young man from Carpathian Russia who spoke Czech, and Yitzhak Nemenczik, an engineer from Kovno, Lithuania, whose wife had been sent to a different Lager with their children.

Dr. Baszni told us about the progress of the war and that our transport was apparently headed to the Mauthausen concentration camp, near Vienna. He suggested that we run away from the theatre hall and offered us assistance. We immediately accepted. It was decided that he would lead us out of the theatre at midnight. We parted in a friendly way with our new saviour and started to prepare for our escape. Our anticipation didn't last long, because when the *Bereichsleiter*, the area manager, of the SS found out about the warm welcome that the residents of Manětín had given us, he ordered that we leave the city in an hour's time.

All the prisoners were ordered to line up in a row outside the theatre hall to get food for a long march. My two friends and I decided not to go with the transport and to run away from the theatre hall instead. But we had a problem: how would we let Dr. Baszni know about this change? There was no time to think. We took advantage of the confusion while the food was being distributed and daringly approached the hall exit, taking only the blankets with us so that we could cover ourselves if we had to sleep outdoors. An elderly SS man was standing at the gate with a gun in his hand; when he asked me where we were going, I boldly answered that we were being sent out to bring more bread and would be right back. The German waved his hand indifferently and told us to go. We hadn't thought that this trick would work so easily. Even now, it is difficult for me to describe the feeling of that moment when my life hung in the balance. As we took our first steps from the tightly guarded hall, we instinctively turned to see if the German was preparing to shoot us.

Once we were out on the narrow street, our hearts felt lighter. The Czechs who noticed us seemed to understand that we had run away, and wished us success in German and in Czech. After we were some distance from the hall, we asked a few residents to inform Dr. Baszni that we had escaped and would await him in the forest a few kilometres away from the town.

It was quite dark by the time we reached the forest, which was on a high hill. From the top of the hill we could observe the town. We sat on the damp grass to rest and consider our situation. We had earlier decided that we would not let on that we were Jews, in case the partisans were Jew-haters. Questions without answers circled in my head. Would our Czech friend know where we were? Would he really be able to help us? It was quiet in the forest, but what would happen if the Germans found us?

Nearly an hour passed. Suddenly we heard shooting coming from the vicinity of the theatre hall. A shiver went through our bones; were the prisoners being shot as they left Manětín? When the sound stopped we tried to sleep, taking turns standing guard. We were so tired that we didn't even pay attention to the damp grass. I don't know how long we slept in this way because time seemed to stop. Suddenly we heard steps and a voice in the distance, calling our names. It was the voice of our saviour, Dr. Zdenek Baszni.

We quickly rose and ran in his direction. We were very happy that we had managed to connect with him despite our unexpectedly early escape. He told us about the evacuation from the theatre hall, that the SS had led everyone away and shot at some who tried to run away. Dr. Baszni was amazed that we had had the courage to run away from the transport.

We followed our guide into the cold, dark night. Crawling on all fours, we cautiously crossed a few bridges that were guarded by Germans. Eventually we reached a hamlet and knocked quietly on the door of a small hut belonging to a member of his partisan group. The owners of the house, the Katsanda family, had been waiting for us. The family consisted of three people: Jozef, or Pepik as he was called by the partisans; his elderly mother; and his young sister, Anetska the shepherdess. They were poor peasants who barely made a living from their small farm and a few cows, yet they were prepared to feed and lodge us. As soon as we entered the house, we found a very large pot of hot water waiting for us so that we could bathe. We were each given clean underwear and then we sat down together at the table to a meal of freshly baked bread and butter and hot milk, which the three of us fell upon like locusts. At 2:00 a.m., we finally went to sleep in the first clean bed with white linens and eiderdown cover we had seen since 1942. In spite of our exhaustion we couldn't fall asleep. It was hard to believe that just a day earlier we had been crawling past armed SS men, and now we were lying in a warm, clean bed.

The next day we discovered that the whole nearby village of Černá Hať belonged to the same partisan group and participated actively in many anti-Nazi sabotage activities. We might have slept all day, but to keep us safe our new saviours woke us after a few hours of sleep and once more led us deep into the forest, a few kilometres from Černá Hať, to a small wooden booth that served as a resting place for Anetska.

Our noble Czech protectors provided us not only with food but, more importantly, with guns and bullets so that we could protect ourselves. Though the booth did not have a window, we could look out through the slits to admire the peacefulness of the forest and watch for SS patrols searching for Czech partisans. Thank God, there were no patrols. Apparently the Germans were afraid to show up here.

The only contact we had with the outside world was through Anetska, who every evening brought us enough food for twenty-four hours. She also provided us with a newspaper published by the Czech anti-Nazi movement, which Morits Kalucz translated for us. Anetska told us that the war would soon end but that we still had to be very careful. We were thrilled by this good news. Even the birds in the forest seemed to rejoice with us; their tweeting and songs reinforced our hope that our suffering would soon end.

We slept in the booth for only one week. The second week we slept at the Katsandas but spent the day in the forest. Every evening the Katsandas led us to their neighbours, the Zelman family, whose two sons also belonged to the same partisan group. The Zelmans prepared a delicious meal for us, and we heard the latest news about the war from their secret radio. Another couple, the Grunslaks, who also wanted to help us, visited the Zelman family while we were there.

We gradually told our Czech saviours about our experience, avoiding mention of our Jewish roots. It is possible they knew that we were Jews, but in no way did they let on. We learned from our new friends that they were part of the team of Czech partisans that included the two Czech soldiers from England who had assassinated the brutal Nazi Reinhard Heydrich, resulting in the Germans destroying the Czech village of Lidice and its whole population in June 1942. They also told us about the deportation of the Czech Jewish population.

At that time, just a few weeks before the end of the war, we did not yet know the full extent of the destruction, and to what degree the Nazis had managed to poison mankind with hatred of one's fellow human beings. We did learn, from this Czech village, that there were those still willing to risk their lives to stand up to the Nazis and protect their victims.

~

One day, we looked through the slits in the booth to see young Anetska running faster than usual. When she reached us, she joyfully shouted that the war had just ended and we were free. We embraced the girl and remained motionless for some time, completely speechless.

That moment on May 8, 1945, will remain in my memory until my last breath. Until we returned to the Katsandas' house, we couldn't believe that our suffering and torment had come to an end and that we were now free of fear, hunger and threat of physical violence. There was a celebratory mood in the whole village, and people kissed one another in the street. Many neighbours gathered in the home of the Katsanda family to celebrate the first day of freedom. We spent two more days with the Katsandas before deciding to head for Prague, the Czech capital.

It was hard to part from our friends, who had shown us so much devotion and warmth. Mrs. Katsanda even asked us to stay a few days longer but we refused. We wanted to get to the capital to seek some means of connecting with our families, though we doubted that any of them had survived.

# Returning

Two days later the three of us arrived in Prague by train. We settled in a hotel that had been prepared for the hundreds of refugees who had been liberated a few days earlier by the Soviet army. It is difficult to describe the joy we saw in Prague. Thousands of Czechs, young and old, gathered in Václavské náměsti, Wenceslas Square, to dance late into the night to the music of orchestras that had come from the surrounding cities. We were swept up in the joyous dancing and thankful for our freedom from Nazi slavery.

A few days later I said farewell to my two friends Nemenczik and Kalucz, who had decided to leave for their hometowns. I remained in Prague, wanting to acquaint myself with the sights of the city and its rich Jewish history. I visited the ghetto, which dates back to the Middle Ages, where the Maharal and Franz Kafka had lived. While strolling on Wenceslas Square I met a former camp inmate from Buchenwald who was Catholic but had belonged to the communist anti-Nazi movement. Five years earlier he had been arrested in Prague by the Germans because of his anti-Nazi activities and sent to the Lager. He invited me to his house and advised me to remain in Prague and begin a new life, even though I revealed to him that I was a Jew.

At the end of May, I was caught up in the enthusiasm of a victory parade in Prague when the Czech army-in-exile marched in under the leadership of General Ludvík Svoboda. As in Manětín and Černá

Hať, the people of Prague showed much understanding for the suffering of the victims of Nazism. In the daily newspapers there was constant reporting of the German occupation. The press described in detail how the SS had organized the deportation of the Jewish population, of which only a small number had been saved. Every day, there were heartbreaking stories about Theresienstadt.

I eventually visited both Theresienstadt and Lidice, two places of martyrdom, with my new Czech friend, Carl. At Lidice, all that remained was a sign bearing the village's name. After the two Czech soldiers had killed Reinhard Heydrich, the Nazis had shot all the men and sent the women and children to concentration camps, where most were killed. They then destroyed all the buildings and burned the town to the ground. All that was left were the charred stones of the burnt houses. Carl burst out crying during our visit.

The following morning I went by myself to Theresienstadt, which the Germans had established for propaganda purposes to show to the world that Jews were being treated fairly. The Lager even had its own bank notes, with which inmates could buy certain products in specially set-up stores. The prisoners were able to organize cultural performances and to educate thousands of children. In June 1944, the Nazis had invited Red Cross representatives to tour Theresienstadt to prove that Jews were not being mistreated, but the truth was that 30,000 perished there and thousands of others were deported to death camps before the Soviet army liberation.

I thought it would be a good idea to remain in Prague. According to the news I was hearing about the antisemitism in Poland, there was no reason to return there. Edvard Beneš had just returned from abroad and would soon be sworn in as the first president of free Czechoslovakia. My friend Carl convinced me to apply to remain in Czechoslovakia. I contacted the office of the president in historic Prague Castle in the Hradčany district and had an interview with President Beneš's secretary. I was received very courteously and promised that I would receive a reply in a few days' time.

I didn't really believe that the president's office would reply to my letter at a time when there was still chaos in the country and there were more important national problems to deal with, but to my great surprise I did receive a positive response. It stated that as a victim of Nazism I had the right to remain in Czechoslovakia and enjoy all the privileges of citizenship. A temporary document allowing me to receive clothing was also enclosed.

The following day I happened to meet Langer, a man from Bratislava whom I had known in Skarżysko. In 1942 he had been deported to Poland with other Czech Jews and later was sent with his wife to Skarżysko. We spent a few hours together, telling one another about our experiences after the deportation from Skarżysko. I learned from him that two women from the Lager in Leipzig, where my friend Hanka and her aunt Esther had been, had returned to Bratislava. I knew these two women, Ila and Erna, quite well and thought that they might know whether Hanka and Esther were still alive.

Though I didn't know their address, I wrote a letter to the Jewish Committee in Bratislava and asked that it be given to the women. A few days after sending the letter I suddenly got sick. I ran a high fever and was coughing so much that I couldn't sleep. When I finally went to the hospital for a medical examination, the doctors kept me there. They diagnosed my lungs as inflamed, likely a result of the long march on snow-covered roads from Berga.

As I lay in the hospital I thought about how lonely I was. At night I dreamed about my family, murdered by the Nazis. I still believed it would be best for me to remain in Czechoslovakia rather than return to Poland, the land of my birth, where the earth was soaked with the blood of innocent Jewish victims. But I remembered the promise I had given Hanka and Esther when we parted in Leipzig that if we survived the war we would meet in Tarnów. When I left the hospital two weeks later, I received a letter from Bratislava stating that Hanka and Esther were already in Tarnów, waiting for me.

I packed up my few belongings and took the train the next day.

At that time there was no direct line to Tarnów and I had to change trains in Katowice, where it was my bad luck to be robbed. Pickpockets stole all my documents and the money I had managed to save since the day of the liberation, so that when I arrived in Tarnów, I didn't even have the money to pay for a taxi. I had to go to my friends' residence on foot.

As I walked along I pictured how the town must have looked before the war. While an active Jewish community had existed here, as I now trudged through the streets I didn't see any signs of Jewish life. The stores that had once belonged to Jews were boarded up; here and there was a sign with the name of the Jewish owner, of whom nothing remained.

Exhausted, I finally made it to 15 Widok Street. I knocked at the door of a small hut to ask for the two Jewish women who had just returned from Germany. An old gentile woman replied in a trembling voice that no Jews lived there. At first I didn't understand why she said this; only later did I realize that she thought I was a member of the Armia Krajowa, illegal factions of which had terrorized and even killed Jews who had returned from the camps. The first meeting with my friends was especially warm. We cried with happiness that we had all survived the war. I remained in Tarnów for a few days and we spoke non-stop about our experiences since we had last seen each other.

Meanwhile, survivors from various camps began to arrive in Tarnów, many of them hoping to find a living relative, but rarely did that happen. Hanka hoped that her father, Yosef, would return from the Soviet Union, where he had fled when the Nazi armies marched into Poland. A friend of her father's brought the tragic news that he had died in a train accident on the way to Siberia. Our losses brought us closer, and Hanka and I eventually decided to marry in Lodz as soon as I found living quarters and a job.

Ten days later, I said goodbye and headed for Lodz to prepare for our new home. There was no doubt in my mind now that we would remain in Poland, where our families had lived for generations. We dreamed of carrying on the chain of our Jewish existence here despite the devastation.

When I got off the train in Lodz my heart was racing. I thought that maybe I'd meet someone I knew here, a relative perhaps. The next morning I decided to ride over to Żeromski Street to see who was living in the residence we had left so many years before. I hoped to be able to get back at least some furniture to help us set up our home. When I knocked at the door of 44 Żeromski Street, an elderly gentile man opened the door and told me that nothing of ours remained. He didn't even allow me to step inside. I felt so hurt from the encounter that I left right away. I even worried that someone might pursue me and harm me.

At that time, many survivors were streaming into Lodz and it was becoming harder to find a place to live. Everyone was afraid to demand the return of their properties from the new owners. In some cases, the original Jewish owners were murdered when they returned to their old homes. Elsewhere, in the streets, Jews were attacked by antisemitic gangs.

Though survivors were returning to reconstruct their lives, I unfortunately found none of my extended family. I went to the newly formed Jewish Committee every day to search for anyone I knew on the list of the new arrivals in Lodz. After a few days I found the name Mordecai Zunshein. He was a friend of the family and also the brother-in-law of my friend Hirsh Tochterman, who had died in Werk C in Skarżysko. Mordecai had survived the war with his wife and was living in Warsaw. I felt it my duty to go there to tell them how Hirsh had died.

I left for Warsaw the very next day and was very warmly welcomed by Hirsh's sister Layke and her husband. I spent three days with them, talking the whole time about our wartime experiences. Mordecai Zunshein came from a fine religious family in the city of my birth, Chmielnik. He was active in the Jewish community in

Chmielnik and later in Staszów, where he married in the 1920s. At the outbreak of the war and when our family arrived in Staszów, Mordecai and my father renewed their friendship. Mordecai told me stories of my father's life, how, in spite of his religious upbringing, he became a teacher in the Jewish *Folks Shule* and the first registrar of the Yiddish Theatre in Chmielnik.

After the first deportation of the Jewish population at the end of 1942, Mordecai, Layke and their ten-year-old son, Lolek, ran away and hid at a peasant's place. They remained with the peasant for a few months until they ran out of money to pay him. By then the Nazi destruction machine was in full swing, with transports going day and night to their final destination – Treblinka, Auschwitz, Sobibor and other places of death.

Feeling desperate, Mordecai did not know where to go with his wife and child. Then, as I mentioned earlier, the Germans announced that a *Judenstaat* was being formed in Sandomierz and those who voluntarily came forward to go there would be able to move about freely. In spite of their experience since the occupation, hundreds of families were drawn into this trap and streamed to Sandomierz, believing in a change in German policy. Mordecai went with his wife and child to Sandomierz as well. When the Germans and their Ukrainian helpers rounded everyone up and loaded them on trains, locking the doors, heart-rending screams were heard. The train travelled through the night. "We knew right away," Mordecai told me, "that we were being taken to Treblinka to be put to death." He got the idea of trying to escape from the moving train through the roof. With the help of a few other men, using their bare hands, he succeeded in prying away a few boards. A few young people, among them Mordecai, Layke and Lolek, thereby managed to escape, easing themselves down as the train slowed.

Luck was with them and they weren't shot by the SS. When they finally reached shelter, they learned that Treblinka was just five kilometres away. They had escaped death by mere minutes. They hid in the forests until the end of the war; tragically, a few months before the Red Army marched into the region, Lolek was shot by a German.

As soon as Warsaw was liberated, Mordecai and his wife went there and, together with Dr. Emil Sommerstein, who had been a Sejm deputy during the pre-war years, formed the Central Committee of Polish Jews to help the survivors. The financial help distributed by the newly formed committee came from the Hebrew Immigrant Aid Society (HIAS).

I spent three days with the Zunshein family, sharing with them my experiences of the war years. It was from them that I heard more about my father and his last days in Staszów. Mordecai had even talked with my father about the new situation and remembered his mood. He told me that my father was convinced that there would be a total elimination of the Jews.

As I returned to Lodz by train, I spent the whole time thinking about my family and trying to understand how I had been able to avoid their fate. It was my destiny to live and continue a Jewish life, but I didn't know what work to do nor how to start a new life in the ruins of Poland.

~

On my return to Lodz I bumped into two friends from Skarżysko, Yamen and Lenchner, who told me that they had been liberated in January 1945 while I was still in the concentration camp in Germany. Over a cup of tea, I learned how they had avoided being sent to Buchenwald. They had run away with the Lager leadership on the night of July 31, 1944, but separated themselves from the rest of the group and, with a few others, took off in a different direction. A few minutes later they heard powerful shooting. The following day they found out that the Ukrainian *Werkschutz* had shot the *Kommandantin* and the whole group with her. They also told me that my friend Natek Neugarten had escaped with them. I was overjoyed to hear that Natek had survived the war and was in Poland.

My friends offered me employment as a bookkeeper in their business. Right after the entry of the Soviet army into Lodz, they opened a café, bakery and restaurant business for the Russian and Polish military. It bore the Russian name *Voentarg*, military exchange. I accepted their offer at once and started my new position a few days later. Though the proprietors of the business were Jews, nearly all the employees were gentile except for me and Hellman, who came from Częstochowa. The working conditions were satisfactory and the pay was relatively good.

I was so happy with my new job that I immediately wrote a letter to my *bashert*, soulmate, in Tarnów, telling her that I had acquired a job as well as a temporary place to live. When she responded a few days later, we decided that our wedding would take place in Lodz in October. It was strange to think that I would soon marry Hanka, with whom I had experienced such tragedy, in the absence of our closest family. Nevertheless I was happy that our dream of being together after the war would soon be realized.

A few days later, as I returned from work, I happened to meet two cousins who had arrived in Lodz some time earlier. I didn't think that they had survived, but Abush Parizer, who was born in Lodz, had survived in Warsaw thanks to his Aryan appearance and false papers. He managed to get back the family's dwelling, which had been occupied by a gentile family. His wife, Hanke, the daughter of my cousin Efraim Zyngier from Staszów, had also survived because of her Aryan appearance. A common destiny bound them together romantically and they got married immediately after the war. Our meeting moved us to tears; we spent all night telling each other how we had managed to survive the war. They told me that when I left for Skarżysko in October 1942, they were both still with their families in Staszów, but a few days later Hanke and her brother David were sent to a labour camp, where David died within a few months.

At the same time that Hanke managed to escape to Warsaw with false identity papers, her cousin Abush also managed to escape from

Staszów with his whole family. The family, consisting of six people, had survived in Warsaw on false documents. They managed to get accommodation outside the Warsaw ghetto. Life was dangerous because if a Pole recognized you as Jewish, he could hand you over to the Germans. Still, they managed to fool the angel of death for some time.

By 1943, the life of the Parizer family was more or less stable. Abush's brother David managed to trade a little and provided food for the whole family. However, after the ghetto uprising, the Nazis came up with another idea of how to lure Jews out of hiding. Nazi collaborators sold false documents, foreign passports and even travel tickets that would apparently allow Jews to leave Poland as South American citizens. The news of these passports spread like wildfire in the Polish capital, and the documents were sold out in a very short time. The payment had to be made in foreign currency, preferably in dollars. Of course, not every Jew in hiding could afford such a luxury, but people did everything they possibly could to be able to leave Poland.

Abush told me that at this time his youngest sister, Manyeh, who was just seventeen years old, became ill with typhus. The family found itself in a dilemma: she would have to be admitted to hospital under an Aryan name, but what would happen if someone recognized her as a Jew, in spite of her non-Jewish appearance? Manyeh was blond and spoke an impeccable Polish, yet everyone worried about her. It didn't occur to anyone in the hospital that Manyeh was Jewish, but when her health deteriorated, she ran to an open window, shouted, "I am a Jew," and jumped out, falling from the fifth floor to her death.

After Manyeh's death, David Parizer purchased the passports. Their best friends did likewise, though they had been hidden in safe places where they could have remained until the end of the war. David was able to get only four passports – for himself; his sister Fela; her husband, Moishe; and their child, Esther. Abush would unfortunately have to remain. He calmed them all by saying that he was prepared to live in Warsaw and perhaps they would all reunite soon.

They were drawn into the Nazi trick. Two weeks later, Polish- and German-language notices were posted in the streets stating that all those who had foreign passports should come with their baggage to the Hotel Polski, from where they would be transported to a ship to sail to their new homelands. The new "South Americans" were delighted. People hauled their suitcases to the hotel. Those who could not afford to acquire the foreign documents envied those who had managed to do so. Among the hidden Jews who were entrapped were the great poet Itzhak Katzenelson and his son. His wife and two young children had perished in Treblinka a few months before. During the Warsaw Ghetto Uprising the poet and his young son were rescued by friends who got them Honduran passports and smuggled them out of the ghetto. He, too, was fooled into going to the Hotel Polski. Before their departure the Jewish "guests" received the very best treatment at the hotel, and so it did not occur to anyone that they were being led to their death.

On the day of departure the guests were picked up by elegant buses and taken to the train station, from where they were to travel to the port city of Gdynia. The German press in Warsaw described how they had left for "home" by boat, and for a long time people believed in the well-planned lie. In reality, the transport of Jews from Hotel Polski was taken to Bergen-Belsen or to the Vittel Lager in France, from where they were later sent to their deaths in Auschwitz.

Then Abush met his future wife, our mutual cousin Hanke, who had also lived in Warsaw on false papers. He told me that he was arranging living quarters so that when his three brothers who had gone to the Soviet Union returned, they would have a roof over their heads. He was completing a military course that would take another six months and offered to let me stay with him until his brothers returned. I moved into his large quarters, which were located near my place of work, and began to prepare for the wedding.

Hanka and her aunt Esther came to Lodz soon thereafter, and the date for the wedding was set for October 14, 1945. Our problem was now finding a *minyan*, a quorum of ten men for a prayer service, or at least a few relatives and friends with whom to share our simcha. We finally put together a list of survivor friends and acquaintances, and I managed to connect with my friend Natek through Yamen and Lenchner. Natek was in a Polish military school in Gdynia. When we met a few days prior to the wedding, he told me about his escape from Skarżysko under a hail of Ukrainian bullets and how he had survived in the forest for several months among Polish partisans.

Right before my wedding, the Jewish Committee in Lodz informed me that my aunt Alte Shar had just arrived in the city from Chmielnik. She and her five children had managed to escape the bloody *Aktion* in Chmielnik and find shelter with a Polish family named Kaszuba in the village of Żydówek, a few kilometres from Chmielnik.

The wedding took place in the comfortable dwelling of our cousins. It's hard, after so many years, to convey the feelings of that evening – we had all gone through so much suffering that we never imagined we would not only emerge alive from the Nazi nightmare, but would also be free people, able to celebrate life. As the rabbi performed the ceremony under the chuppah, the wedding canopy, Hanka and I both felt that the souls of our parents were present and celebrating with us.

After the wedding, we remained with our cousins and gradually began to settle into our new life. We believed that, after such a great catastrophe, we'd be able to live free of Polish antisemitism because we thought that the Polish people had learned from their experience under the Nazis and would treat us with tolerance and humanity. Unfortunately, the reality was different. As the survivors returned to Poland, they felt unwanted. Their homes were occupied by families who kept the valuables entrusted to them for safekeeping. Armed attacks on Jews occurred in several cities in Poland.

I figured that this was just a passing moment in the new democratic Poland and went about my daily activities. I worked five days per week and enjoyed my job. We had the company of new friends and acquaintances. It didn't even occur to us to think of leaving Poland, until an incident changed our fate. One Monday morning, I arrived at work at nine o'clock as usual. The head bookkeeper in the office, Sasnowski, a captain in the Polish army, usually started work at the same hour. This day, however, he would not arrive until an hour later. I had not been at work long before there was a knock on my office door. When I opened it, a man with a revolver in his hand entered and said to me, "I know there is a Jew employed here. You must show me who he is, or you will be the victim. The new Poland does not need any Jews, and since Hitler didn't manage to kill all the Jews, we will do so!"

I was dumbstruck and almost fainted. I understood that he meant the director of the restaurant, Hellman, but I had to control myself and say something so as to not arouse suspicion that I was also a Jew. It took some time to convince him that no Jews were working in *Voentarg* at all. When my co-worker Captain Sasnowski later arrived, he saw my pale face and understood that something had happened. He tried to calm me down and assure me that democratic Poland knew what to do with the enemies of socialism. But I couldn't listen to what the captain was telling me. I could only think that, just a few months after the Nazis had been defeated, there still existed Polish people who wanted to complete what Hitler hadn't.

My wife and I had returned to Poland with the idea of renewing our broken lives only to once again fear getting killed, this time by a Polish bullet. When I went home after work and told Hanka about the incident, we decided that we could not remain in Poland. Now the problem was where to go and how to get an exit permit.

We heard that the Allied armies had set up displaced persons (DP) camps, maintained by the United Nations Relief and Rehabilitation Administration (UNRRA). The camps served as gathering points for immigration to Western democratic countries. I was able to buy a false Soviet permit to go by train to Berlin.

At the end of November 1945, we said farewell to friends and acquaintances and prepared for departure. It was hard for me to leave my job and the comfortable living quarters we shared with our cousins. Nevertheless, we left Lodz with a group of friends and headed for Berlin. We felt as though we were escaping from a fire as the train neared the German border. When Polish and Russian military officers checked our travel documents, we prayed that our false papers should pass *b'shalom*, safely. Many passengers were indeed detained, and we don't know what happened to them. We, on the contrary, were lucky. When the Polish soldier examined our baggage and documents, I treated him to a bottle of vodka that I had taken along especially in case of need. The bottle of vodka worked, and no one else in our compartment was inspected.

Slowly, the train continued on its way across the Polish-German border.

# A New Beginning

When I left Prague for Poland, I never imagined that I would again be forced to tread on German soil. In Berlin, the UNRRA handled the massive influx of former concentration camp inmates. We were settled in quite a comfortable hotel, where we met many Polish Jews who, like us, had run away from the antisemitism in Poland. We remained in the hotel for a week and rejoiced at the ruins of Berlin. We didn't wish to remain in Germany but instead intended to join a group of survivors and immigrate to a country that would accept us and let us live as free people.

We finally went to the Landsberg DP camp, not far from Munich. On our arrival we found hundreds of Jews already there. The DP camp was in a former German military barracks and financed by the international organization, but the inner administration was in the hands of survivors. Landsberg had its own police and hospital, as well as a Jewish newspaper which, for lack of Yiddish typeset, had to use the Latin. The camp served as a transit centre offering the opportunity for immigration to Western countries.

Because of the crowding and the steady arrival of additional refugees, we had to share a room with two other people who had been with us in Skarżysko. Every day, people gathered near the administration building, where the latest list of inhabitants who were being searched for was posted. Relatives from abroad searched for survivors in this way. There were cases of survivors connecting with their relatives in America, who made the necessary preparations for legal immigration. At one point, one of my American cousins, who happened to be serving in the American army not far from Munich, visited us. We wanted to go to the United States and had even registered in the appropriate office.

At the same time, groups of different political leanings formed to prepare for illegal immigration to Palestine. A group of German and Austrian survivors from the transit camps did manage to arrive safely in the Holy Land, but the greatest number were prevented by the British from landing there and were instead sent to internment camps in Cyprus.

During the first months of 1946, the leaders of the Yishuv, the Jewish community, in Eretz Israel started to visit the DP camps. Among them was David Ben Gurion, who became the first prime minister of Israel. He spoke with the survivors, sharing with them the feelings of the people of Eretz Israel about the loss of six million during the war.

Though we thought that we wouldn't be in Landsberg for long, I didn't want to sit idly. I was successful in getting a job as the leader of the provisions post in the hospital. The administrators of the hospital, including the doctors and nurses, were all Jewish. Most of the patients were those who had been sick when they came out of the camps. Every day, new patients arrived on transports from Poland and Russia, and the hospital was soon overflowing. My greatest satisfaction was when, after the destruction of my people, the first Jewish babies were born in the hospital.

Soon, a choir and a drama group – in which I participated – were formed. Concerts took place nearly weekly, and the crowd waited eagerly for every cultural event, taking much pleasure in hearing a Yiddish word. We also performed in other DP camps near Landsberg and in the theatre in Munich.

Then we learned that Hanka was pregnant. We both accepted this news with mixed feelings: we were pleased that we could bring forth a new generation but worried about where we would immigrate to establish a stable life.

Some individuals had already received the necessary documentation from their relatives abroad for eventual immigration, but we had no address for any relatives. One day, I happened to see the name Yitzhok Gerstenkorn in the Landsberg newspaper and realized that this must be my father's cousin who had left Warsaw for Eretz Israel in 1923. He had been with a group of religious Jews who founded the colony Bnei Brak, which over time had developed as a religious centre near Tel Aviv. At the very time that we were in the camps, Yitzhok Gerstenkorn was the mayor of Bnei Brak.

I was so excited at the thought that my wife and I might be able to reach the Holy Land. I immediately sent my cousin a letter through a representative in the Jewish Brigade, a wartime battalion that was helping Jews after the war. A few weeks later I received a reply from a different cousin writing on his behalf. He wrote how happy they were to hear that we had survived but advised me not to come just yet to the Holy Land because of the economic difficulties there. Once again, we worried about where to go.

In the summer of 1946, more Jews arrived in Landsberg from Poland after the Kielce pogrom, in which about forty innocent Jewish victims were murdered because of a false report about a child being kidnapped by a Jew. My aunt Alte Shar and her five children arrived in the last group. Having relatives with us cheered us up a bit; we hoped that all of us would be able to immigrate somewhere together. One day, I noticed my name on the list of names at the office – someone was searching for me! It was my uncle Yehoshua Teiflboim from Paris, France. It had never occurred to me that he would be among the living. He had left Poland for France because of the difficult economic times in Poland at the start of the 1930s.

I contacted him, and it didn't take long before he arrived in Landsberg. It's difficult to describe our first meeting, in the presence of my wife and aunt and her five children. Uncle told us how he and his wife had escaped through the window of their home in Paris when the French police knocked on their door. He suggested that we come to Paris to build our life anew, but we decided to wait until after the birth of our child to decide. When we said goodbye to my uncle several days later, we promised to stay in close contact.

Our son Yitzhak (Isaac) was born on August 16, 1946, and I was overjoyed that he would carry the name of my father. It is ironic that our child was born in Landsberg, the very city where Hitler wrote his master plan of genocide, *Mein Kampf,* and in the same hospital where he had been a patient during his imprisonment. Maybe it was destiny that my wife and I should survive and come to Landsberg, so that our son could be born where Hitler had planned to destroy all the Jews.

When, in the autumn months of 1946, people were immigrating to various countries, our turn also came to decide where to go. Since it would take a very long time to get into the United States, we accepted the invitation of our uncle Yehoshua and decided to leave for Paris. Because we didn't have the proper legal documents, we would have to reach Paris illegally. When our son was six weeks old, a French army transport truck came to our place to take us on the long road to Paris.

It was a cool evening when we said goodbye to friends. We left, hoping to finally start a new life far from the cursed German soil.

# Epilogue

In 1946, David and Anna (Hanka) crossed into France in the back of a truck, without documentation and with me, a hidden baby to shush. Making their way to Paris, they found Uncle Charles (Yehoshua) and Auntie Fela in the Marais Quarter, in a fourth-floor walk-up on Rue du Roi-de-Sicile, minutes away from Rue des Rosiers and a lovely synagogue.

Uncle Charles happily took in his beloved family and taught David basic skills as a *Schneider*, a tailor. Life was good, with summers at the beach and on a farm. But in cramped quarters and with David needing new opportunities, he and Anna decided to immigrate to Canada, where his friend Liebel Ofshany was able to sponsor them. The crossing of the Atlantic on the *General Taylor* – arriving at Pier 21 in Halifax on April 1, 1951 – was not quite a Carnival Cruise, but the port of call was worth the journey: our home, Canada, and the sight of my very first snow.

The image that lingers in my mind, and that is reinforced by many family photos and videos, is that of David and Anna Newman dancing at family celebrations and laughing with the many friends they made for nearly six decades after the war. Although Anna often expressed a nostalgic longing for the simplicity of the pre-war years, this belied the fact that, with her beloved husband, David, she spent "fifty-six happy years" ferociously answering the dark shadows of the war by living a meaningful and productive life with family and friends in their wonderful home in Canada.

They celebrated many simchas with their created surrogate extended family, Club Ten, a society of ten couples who had survived the war alone and came to Canada to start anew in Toronto. David and Anna's immediate family grew with the birth of my sister, Gloria (Yochevet); five grandchildren and great-grandchildren followed.

The gifts that David bestowed on the people around him were the gifts of laughter; music (he had a lovely voice); literature; the love of theatre and Yiddish (he was a great stage actor); poetry and thoughtful engagement with ideas about Jewish culture and religion; and the love for Israel and its great achievements in human development.

David Newman taught Yiddish to many loving students, old and young; they still talk about him fondly years after the classes. David co-founded the Kol Yisroel congregation at the Borochov Centre, which still has an active membership, and was referred to as "Mr. Borochov" in articles written after his passing. A staunch Labour Zionist and a lifelong lover of Israel, he received many awards for fundraising and taking part in "Society" meetings to promote Jewish causes. He was the "go to" eulogist for all of Club Ten and could be counted on to speak at any function. There is a collage of photos to be made of David at a microphone. And as a dedicated witness to the Holocaust, he spoke frequently to young students in schools to keep the memory of the Shoah alive.

Anna and David pledged to outlive Hitler when they met in the work camp at Skarżysko. They did that. But the legacy of David Newman was so much more, one of love for his family and a deep love of life.

*Jack Newman, 2015*

# Glossary

**Agudath Israel** (Hebrew; Union of Israel) An Orthodox political organization established in 1912 that stood for elections in Poland. The direction of the party in religious, social and political issues was determined by Torah scholars.

*Aktion* (German; pl. *Aktionen*) The brutal roundup of Jews for forced labour, forcible resettlement into ghettos, mass murder by shooting or deportation to death camps.

**aliyah** (Hebrew; pl. *aliyot*, literally, ascent) A term used by Jews and modern Israelis to refer to Jewish immigration to Israel; the term is also used to refer to "going up" to the altar in a synagogue to read from the Torah.

**antisemitism** Prejudice, discrimination, persecution and/or hatred against Jewish people, institutions, culture and symbols.

**Armia Krajowa** (Polish; in English, Home Army) Also known as AK. Formed in February 1942, the Armia Krajowa was the largest Polish resistance movement in German-occupied Poland during World War II, best known for orchestrating the 1944 Warsaw Uprising. Although the organization has been criticized for antisemitism and some factions were even guilty of killing Jews, it is also true that the AK established a Section for Jewish Affairs that collected information about what was happening to Jews in Poland, centralized contacts between Polish and Jewish military organizations, and supported the Relief Council for Jews in Poland. Between 1942 and 1945, hundreds of Jews joined the AK.

**Aryan** A nineteenth-century anthropological term originally used to refer to the Indo-European family of languages and, by extension, the peoples who spoke them. The term became a synonym for people of Nordic or Germanic descent in the theories that inspired Nazi racial ideology. "Aryan" was an official classification in Nazi racial laws to denote someone of pure Germanic blood, as opposed to "non-Aryans," such as Slavs, Jews, part-Jews, Roma and Sinti, and others of supposedly inferior racial stock.

**Auschwitz** (German; in Polish, Oświęcim) A town in southern Poland approximately forty kilometres from Krakow, it is also the name of the largest complex of Nazi concentration camps that were built nearby. The Auschwitz complex contained three main camps: Auschwitz I, a slave labour camp built in May 1940; Auschwitz II-Birkenau, a death camp built in early 1942; and Auschwitz-Monowitz, a slave labour camp built in October 1942. In 1941, Auschwitz I was a testing site for usage of the lethal gas Zyklon B as a method of mass killing, which then went into wide usage. Between 1942 and 1944, transports arrived at Auschwitz-Birkenau from almost every country in Europe – hundreds of thousands from both Poland and Hungary, and thousands from France, the Netherlands, Greece, Slovakia, Bohemia and Moravia, Yugoslavia, Belgium, Italy and Norway. As well, more than 30,000 people were deported there from other concentration camps. It is estimated that 1.1 million people were murdered in Auschwitz; approximately 950,000 were Jewish; 74,000 Polish; 21,000 Roma; 15,000 Soviet prisoners of war; and 10,000 to 15,000 other nationalities. The Auschwitz complex was liberated by the Soviet army in January 1945.

**Bar Kokhba, Shimon** The leader of the Jewish rebellion against the Roman Empire between 132 and 135 CE, which came to be known as the Bar Kokhba Revolt. Bar Kokhba has been the subject of many novels, plays and operas.

**Beneš, Edvard** (1884–1948) The second and fourth president of Czechoslovakia (1935–38 and 1945–48). After Germany took control of part of Czechoslovakia in 1938, Beneš went into exile in Britain, where he formed the Czechoslovak government-in-exile. After the war, Beneš was reinstated as president until the Communist coup in February 1948; he resigned in June of that year and was succeeded by Communist leader Klement Gottwald.

**Berga** A slave labour camp constructed near Buchenwald in November 1944 to dig tunnels for an underground synthetic oil plant. Berga was evacuated April 10–11, 1945, and its prisoners taken on a death march. The number of survivors is unknown. *See also* Buchenwald.

**blood libel** The false accusation that Jews use the blood of Christian children in preparing matzah for the holiday of Passover. It is one of the most persistent forms of antisemitism in Europe, dating back to the twelfth century.

**Blum, André Léon** (1872–1950) Prime minister of France from June 4, 1936, to June 22, 1937, and March 13, 1938, to April 10, 1938; and president of the provisional government of the French Republic from December 16, 1946, to January 22, 1947. Blum was the first Jew and Socialist to serve as prime minister of France. After the German occupation of France in June 1940, Blum was arrested for treason and in 1943 he was deported to the Buchenwald concentration camp. He was liberated in May 1945 in German-occupied South Tyrol in Italy.

**British Mandate Palestine** The area of the Middle East under British rule from 1923 to 1948, as established by the League of Nations after World War I. During that time, the United Kingdom severely restricted Jewish immigration. The Mandate area encompassed present-day Israel, Jordan, the West Bank and the Gaza Strip.

**Buchenwald** A concentration camp complex located near Weimar,

Germany, that was in operation between July 1937 and April 1945. The Buchenwald complex comprised more than 130 subcamps and an estimated 250,000 prisoners from every country in Europe. The camp was initially established for male prisoners, but women started to arrive at the camp in late 1943 or early 1944. Prisoners were forced to work at over 90 different places for employers in Weimar and its environs. At least 56,000 of 238,980 male inmates are known to have been murdered. Buchenwald was liberated by the US army in April 1945.

**Chmielnicki Uprising** (1648–1649) A series of military campaigns launched by the Cossacks – members of various ethnic groups in southern Russia, Ukraine and Siberia – to free the Ukraine from Polish domination and establish their own rule in the region. Led by Bohdan Chmielnicki (1595–1657), the Cossacks claimed that the Poles had sold them to the Jews as slaves and launched attacks that resulted in an estimated 100,000 deaths and the destruction of almost three hundred Jewish communities.

**chuppah** (Hebrew; literally, covering) The canopy used in traditional Jewish weddings that is usually made of a cloth (sometimes a prayer shawl) stretched or supported over four poles. It is meant to symbolize the home the couple will build together.

**Cyprus** An island nation in the Mediterranean and former British colony that was granted independence from Great Britain in 1960. In the 1940s, Cyprus was the location of British detention camps for European Jewish refugees who were attempting to illegally immigrate to British Mandate Palestine. More than 50,000 Jewish refugees were interned in these camps. *See also* British Mandate Palestine.

**Czarniecki, Stefan** (1599–1665) A Polish-Lithuanian general who helped defend Poland from invasion by Sweden in 1655. His troops attacked the Jewish communities through which they passed, destroying synagogues and killing many people.

**Czerniaków, Adam** (1880–1942) Head of the Warsaw Ghetto Judenrat. Czerniaków committed suicide on July 23, 1942, one day after the Nazis ordered thousands of Jews deported from the ghetto to the Treblinka death camp.

**DP camps** (Displaced Persons camps) Facilities set up by the Allied authorities and the United Nations Relief and Rehabilitation Administration (UNRRA) in October 1945 to resolve the refugee crisis that arose at the end of World War II. The camps provided temporary shelter and assistance to the millions of people – not only Jews – who had been displaced from their home countries as a result of the war and helped them prepare for resettlement. *See also* United Nations Relief and Rehabilitation Administration (UNRRA).

**Frank, Hans** (1900–1946) Nazi governor general of the occupied area in central Poland known as the *Generalgouvernement* from 1939 to 1945. Frank oversaw the establishment of ghettos for Jews and the use of Jewish and Polish civilians for forced labour.

**ghetto** A confined residential area for Jews. The term originated in Venice, Italy, in 1516 with a law requiring all Jews to live on a segregated, gated island known as Ghetto Nuovo. Throughout the Middle Ages in Europe, Jews were often forcibly confined to gated Jewish neighbourhoods. During the Holocaust, the Nazis forced Jews to live in crowded and unsanitary conditions in rundown districts of cities and towns.

**Gustloff Werke** A German munitions firm that operated a series of factories in the 1930s, one of which was built in March 1943 at the Buchenwald concentration camp. *See also* Buchenwald.

*Gymnasium* (German) A word used throughout Central and Eastern Europe to denote high school.

*hachshara* (Hebrew; literally, preparation) A training program to prepare new immigrants for life in the Land of Israel.

**Harvest Festival** The massacre of about 42,000 prisoners in Poniatowa, Trawniki labour camp and Majdanek by SS units on November 3 and 4, 1943, as music was played through loudspeakers.

At Poniatowa, inmates had been previously ordered to dig anti-aircraft trenches; these became the mass graves of approximately 14,000 inmates. *See also* Poniatowa, Majdanek.

**Hashomer Hatzair** (Hebrew; literally, The Youth Guard) A left-wing Zionist youth movement founded in Central Europe in the early twentieth century to prepare young Jews to become workers and farmers, to establish kibbutzim – collective settlements – in pre-state Israel and work the land as pioneers. Before World War II, there were 70,000 Hashomer Hatzair members worldwide; it is the oldest Zionist youth movement still in existence.

**Hasidic Judaism** (from the Hebrew word *hasid*; literally, piety) An Orthodox Jewish spiritual movement founded by Rabbi Israel ben Eliezer in eighteenth-century Poland; characterized by philosophies of mysticism and focusing on joyful prayer. This movement resulted in a new kind of leader who attracted disciples as opposed to the traditional rabbis who focused on the intellectual study of Jewish law. Melody and dance have an important role in Hasidic worship. There are many different sects of Hasidic Judaism, but followers of Hasidism often wear dark, conservative clothes as well as a head covering to reflect modesty and show respect to God.

**Heydrich, Reinhard** (1904–1942) Chief of the Reich Main Security Office (overseeing the SD, the Nazi intelligence service, and the Gestapo) and one of the orchestrators of the "Final Solution," the Nazi plan for the systematic murder of Europe's Jewish population. While serving as *Reichsprotektor* of Czechoslovakia, Heydrich's brutality toward Czech citizens earned him the nickname the "Butcher of Prague." In May 1942, two Czech patriots parachuted in from Britain and attacked Heydrich in Prague by throwing a grenade into his open car; he succumbed to his injuries one week later.

**Jewish Brigade** A battalion that was formed in September 1944 under the command of the British Eighth Army. The Jewish Brigade included more than 5,000 volunteers from Palestine. After the war, the Brigade was essential in helping Jewish refugees and organizing their entry into Palestine. It was disbanded by the British in 1946.

**Judenrat** (German; pl. *Judenräte*) Jewish Council. A group of Jewish leaders appointed by the Germans to administer and provide services to the local Jewish population under occupation and carry out Nazi orders. The *Judenräte*, which appeared to be self-governing entities but were actually under complete Nazi control, faced difficult and complex moral decisions under brutal conditions and remain a contentious subject. The chairmen had to decide whether to comply or refuse to comply with Nazi demands. Some were killed by the Nazis for refusing, while others committed suicide. Jewish officials who advocated compliance thought that cooperation might save at least some of the population. Some who denounced resistance efforts did so because they believed that armed resistance would bring death to the entire community.

**Judenstaat** A Jewish "state" established by the Nazis in Sandomierz in late 1942. This "state" was, in actuality, a ghetto and was liquidated on January 10, 1943; most of its inhabitants were sent to Treblinka while a small group considered able to work were sent to Skarżysko-Kamienna. The Nazis had used the term *Judenstaat* as an ironic reference to Theodor Herzl's 1896 book *Der Judenstaat* (The Jewish State).

**Kaddish** (Aramaic; holy) Also known as the Mourner's Prayer, Kaddish is said as part of mourning rituals in Jewish prayer services as well as at funerals and memorials.

**kapo** (German) A concentration camp prisoner appointed by the SS to oversee other prisoners as slave labourers.

*kehilla* Local, quasi-governmental Jewish communal organizations, comprised of both religious and secular members, that existed throughout Europe and elsewhere during the interwar period.

**Kielce pogrom** The July 1946 riots in a city in Poland where about

250 Jews lived after the war (the pre-war Jewish population had been more than 20,000). After the false report of a young Polish boy being kidnapped by Jews, police arrested and beat Jewish residents in the city, inciting a mob of hundreds of Polish civilians to violently attack and kill forty Jews while police stood by. Combined with other post-war antisemitic incidents throughout Poland – other pogroms occurred in Rzeszów, Krakow, Tarnów and Sosnowiec, and robberies and blackmail were common – this event was the catalyst for a mass exodus: between July 1945 and September 1946, more than 80,000 Jews left Poland.

**Koch, Ilse** (1906–1967) An SS-*Aufseherin*, overseer, at Buchenwald concentration camp, where her husband, Karl-Otto Koch, was commandant. Koch was known for her cruelty and, after the war ended, was sentenced to life imprisonment for her crimes. Koch committed suicide in September 1967.

**Koch, Karl-Otto** (1897–1945) First commandant of the Sachsenhausen concentration camp and of Buchenwald (1937 to 1941). In August 1943, the Nazi Party charged Koch with murder and a variety of criminal offenses; he was executed in April 1945.

**Kristallnacht** (German; literally, Night of Broken Glass) A series of pogroms that took place in Germany and Austria between November 9 and 10, 1938. Over the course of twenty-four hours, ninety-one Jews were murdered, 25,000 to 30,000 were arrested and deported to concentration camps, two hundred synagogues were destroyed and thousands of Jewish businesses and homes were ransacked. Planned by the Nazis as a coordinated attack on the Jews of Germany and Austria, Kristallnacht is often seen as an important turning point in Hitler's policies of systematic persecution of Jews.

*Lagerführer* (German) Commander of a concentration camp.

**Landsberg Prison** A facility in Landsberg am Lech, Bavaria, where Adolf Hitler was held after being convicted for treason in 1924. During his short incarceration, Hitler wrote *Mein Kampf*. After the war, Nazis convicted at the Dachau and Nuremberg War Crimes Trials were held in Landsberg, pending their execution for crimes against humanity. See also *Mein Kampf.*

*landsleit* (Yiddish; in English, landsman) A member of a group who comes from the same town.

*Lebensraum* (German; literally, living space) Additional territory the Nazis believed they needed for nationalist and economic purposes.

**Majdanek** A concentration camp in Lublin, Poland, in operation from October 1941 to July 1944, when it was liberated by the Soviet army. More than 60,000 Jewish prisoners died at the camp.

**Markiel, Jacob (Jacques)** (1911–2008) A Polish-Jewish French artist, Markiel was held in Drancy, Auschwitz and Buchenwald. Markiel's talent helped him survive the war and after liberation he returned to Paris, where he continued to paint.

**Mauthausen** A notoriously brutal Nazi concentration camp located about twenty kilometres east of the Austrian city of Linz. First established in 1938, it grew to encompass fifty nearby subcamps and became the largest forced labour complex in the German-occupied territories. By the end of the war, close to 200,000 prisoners had passed through the Mauthausen forced labour camp system and almost 120,000 of them died there – including 38,120 Jews – from starvation, disease and hard labour. The US army liberated the camp on May 5, 1945.

*Mein Kampf* (German; *My Struggle*) Adolf Hitler's manifesto for his National Socialist movement that appeared in two volumes in 1925 and 1926 (though the second volume was dated 1927). The book combines autobiography with a delineation of Hitler's racist, antisemitic, ultra-nationalist, anti-democratic and anti-Marxist ideology. It was widely disseminated across Germany following Hitler's rise to power in 1933. Today, the book is considered hate speech and selling or trading it is restricted in many countries.

*minyan* (Hebrew) The quorum of ten adult male Jews required for certain religious rites. The term can also designate a congregation.

**Mizrachi** (Hebrew; acronym of Merkaz Ruchani; in English, spiritual centre) An Orthodox nationalist Zionist movement founded in Vilna, Lithuania, in 1902. Mizrachi was founded on the belief that the Torah is central to Zionism and Jewish life. The movement's principles are encompassed in its slogan "The land of Israel for the people of Israel according to the Torah of Israel."

*Muselmann* (German; Muslim) A slang term used by camp prisoners to describe prisoners who were near death and seemed to have lost the will to live. Some scholars attribute the use of the word to the fact that the prostrate and dying prisoners were reminiscent of devout Muslims at prayer.

*numerus clausus* (Latin; closed number) A quota limiting admission to institutions or professions. In nineteenth and twentieth-century Eastern Europe, Jews were frequently restricted from entering universities, professional associations and public administration.

*Obersturmführer* (German; senior storm leader) A Nazi military rank. Within the SS, the role of the *Obersturmführer* could vary from Gestapo officer to concentration camp supervisor.

*Ordnungsdienst* (German; literally, Order Service) The Jewish ghetto police force established by the Jewish Councils on the orders of the Germans. The force was armed with clubs and was created to carry out various tasks in the ghettos, such as traffic control and guarding the ghetto gates. Eventually, some policemen also participated in rounding up Jews for forced labour and transportation to the death camps. There has been much debate and controversy surrounding the role of both the Jewish Councils and the Jewish police. Even though the Jewish police exercised considerable power within the ghetto, to the Germans these policemen were still Jews and subject to the same fate as other Jews. *See also* Judenrat.

**Piłsudski, Józef** (1867–1935) Leader of the Second Polish Republic from 1926 to 1935. Piłsudski was largely responsible for achieving Poland's independence in 1918 after more than a century of being partitioned by Russia, Austria and Prussia. Piłsudski's regime was notable for improving the lot of ethnic minorities, including Poland's large Jewish population. Many Polish Jews felt that his regime was key to keeping the antisemitic currents in Poland in check; when he died in 1935, the quality of life of Poland's Jews deteriorated once again.

**Pister, Hermann** (1885–1948) SS-*Oberführer* and commandant at Buchenwald concentration camp between January 1942 and April 1945. In 1947, Pister was sentenced to death in a war crimes trial. He died of a heart attack in Landsberg Prison in September 1948. *See also* Landsberg Prison.

**Płaszów** A labour camp constructed on two Jewish cemeteries in a suburb of Krakow in 1942 and enlarged to become a concentration camp in January 1944. Płaszów was also used as a transit camp – more than 150,000 people passed through the camp, many en route to Auschwitz. About 80,000 were murdered in the camp itself, either by execution or through hard labour. By mid-1944, Płaszów held more than 20,000 prisoners; inmates were used for slave labour in the quarry or railway construction and were subject to the volatile whims of camp commandant Amon Göth, who was personally responsible for more than 8,000 deaths.

**Poalei Zion** (Hebrew; also Poale Zion; Workers of Zion) A Marxist-Jewish Zionist movement founded in the Russian Empire in the early twentieth century.

**Poniatowa** A town in southeastern Poland that was the site of a concentration camp between 1941 and 1943, when it was incorporated into the Majdanek concentration camp. Poniatowa was initially established to hold Soviet P O W s, about 20,000 of whom perished there by 1942. The camp was later expanded to include workshops where Jewish slave labourers, first transported there in October 1942, made army uniforms. The mainly Jewish workforce was massacred in the so-called Harvest Festival in November 1943. *See also* Harvest Festival.

**Poznański, Izrael** (1833–1900) A Polish textile manufacturer and philanthropist who transformed a small two-storey building in Lodz into a palace and factory that served for a time as the family home. In 2006, the building was restored and converted into a museum called the Manufaktura Centre.

**Przytyk pogrom** (1936) A boycott of Jewish market traders that escalated into a riot and resulted in the deaths of a non-Jewish Pole and a Jewish couple. More than twenty people were beaten and dozens of Jewish apartments and shops were attacked and destroyed.

**Reichstag** The German parliament. When arsonists burned the building on February 27, 1933, Nazis accused Communists of setting the fire and many Communist members of parliament were arrested. The day after, the Decree of the Reich President for the Protection of People and State (more commonly known as the Reichstag Fire Decree) was passed, which suspended the right to assembly, freedom of speech, freedom of the press and other constitutional protections, including all restraints on police investigations. The passage of the decree was an essential step in establishing the Third Reich as a one-party totalitarian state.

**Reschke, Erich** (1902–1980) Communist leader who joined the German communist party in 1920 and was active in the fight against Nazism. Arrested for his activities in 1933, he spent five years at Lichtenburg camp before being transferred to the Buchenwald concentration camp, where he was a kapo and a camp elder.

**Rydz-Śmigły, Edward** (1886–1941) Marshal of Poland and Commander-in-Chief of Poland's armed forces until Poland fell to the Germans in 1939.

**Rosh Hashanah** (Hebrew; New Year) The autumn holiday that marks the beginning of the Jewish year and ushers in the High Holy Days. It is observed by a synagogue service that ends with the blowing of the *shofar* (ram's horn), which marks the beginning of the holiday. The service is usually followed by a family dinner where sweet foods, such as apples and honey, are eaten to symbolize and celebrate a sweet new year.

**Schlieben** A town in the eastern part of Germany that was the site of the Schlieben-Berga concentration camp, a forced labour sub-camp of Buchenwald that existed from July 1944 to April 1945. Inmates manufactured chemicals for shells and anti-tank weapons, and assembled metal tubes filled with explosives. During the nine months that the camp existed, about 195 prisoners died.

**Shabbes** (Yiddish; in English, Sabbath) The weekly day of rest beginning Friday at sunset and ending Saturday after nightfall, ushered in by the lighting of candles on Friday night and the recitation of blessings over wine and challah (egg bread); a day of celebration as well as prayer, it is customary to eat three festive meals, attend synagogue services and refrain from doing any work or travelling.

**shtetl** (Yiddish; small town) A small village or town with a predominantly Jewish population that existed before World War II in Central and Eastern Europe, where life revolved around Judaism and Judaic culture. In the Middle Ages, Jews were not allowed to own land, and so the shtetl developed as a refuge for Jews.

***Shulamith*** A Yiddish operetta, also known as *The Daughter of Jerusalem*, that was written by Abraham Goldfaden in 1880 or 1881.

***sifrei* Torah** (Hebrew; Torah scrolls) The Torah is the Five Books of Moses (the first five books of the Bible), also called the Pentateuch. It is the core of Jewish scripture, traditionally believed to have been given to Moses on Mount Sinai. In Christianity it is referred to as the "Old Testament." Sections of the handwritten scroll of the Torah are read during synagogue services on the Jewish Sabbath.

**simcha** (Hebrew; gladness, joy) Generally refers to a festive occasion.

**Skarżysko-Kamienna** A town in east-central Poland that also became the site of a Nazi forced labour camp after the town's entire Jewish population was deported to the Treblinka death camp in 1942. Between October 1942 and August 1, 1944, when the camp was dissolved, 25,000 to 30,000 Jews were brought to Skarżysko-Kamienna; 18,000 to 23,000 of them died there.

**Sommerstein, Dr. Emil** (1883–1957) A Polish-born lawyer who served in the Polish lower house of parliament from 1922 to 1927 and 1929 to 1939, and participated in the founding conference of the World Jewish Conference in 1936. After surviving the war years in the Soviet Union, he became the first chairman of the Central Committee of Polish Jews, which helped to rebuild Jewish life in Poland.

**Star of David** (in Hebrew, *Magen David*) The six-pointed star that is the ancient and most recognizable symbol of Judaism. During World War II, Jews in Nazi-occupied areas were frequently forced to wear a badge or armband with the Star of David on it as an identifying mark of their lesser status and to single them out as targets for persecution.

**Strigler, Mordechai** (1921–1998) Writer, poet and editor of the Yiddish-language New York-based newspaper *The Forward*. During the war, Strigler fought in the Warsaw Ghetto Uprising and was later imprisoned in several concentration camps, including Majdanek and Buchenwald. At Buchenwald, he gave Yiddish and Hebrew lessons to Jewish children, joined the underground resistance and organized literary evenings.

**Sudetenland** The western border region of former Czechoslovakia that was inhabited primarily by ethnic Germans before World War II. In an attempt to prevent World War II, Britain, France and Italy agreed to the annexation of the Sudetenland by the Third Reich as part of the Munich Agreement, which was signed on September 30, 1938.

**Svoboda, Ludvík** (1895–1979) Czechoslovak general who fought in both world wars and served as president of Czechoslovakia from 1968 to 1975.

**Swedish invasion of Poland** The series of invasions of the Polish-Lithuanian Commonwealth by Sweden between 1655 and 1660.

**Theresienstadt** (German; in Czech, Terezín) A walled town in the Czech Republic sixty kilometres north of Prague that served as both a ghetto and a concentration camp. More than 73,000 Jews from the German Protectorate of Bohemia and Moravia and from the Greater German Reich (including Austria and parts of Poland) were deported to Theresienstadt between 1941 and 1945, 60,000 of whom were deported to Auschwitz or other death camps. Theresienstadt was showcased as a "model" ghetto for propaganda purposes to demonstrate to delegates from the International Red Cross and others the "humane" treatment of Jews and to counter information reaching the Allies about Nazi atrocities and mass murder. Theresienstadt was liberated on May 8, 1945, by the Soviet Red Army.

**Treaty of Non-Aggression between Germany and the USSR** The treaty that was signed on August 24, 1939, and was colloquially known as the Molotov-Ribbentrop Pact, after signatories Soviet foreign minister Vyacheslav Molotov and German foreign minister Joachim von Ribbentrop. The main provisions of the pact stipulated that the two countries would not go to war with each other and that they would both remain neutral if either one was attacked by a third party. One of the key components of the treaty was the division of various independent countries – including Poland – into Nazi and Soviet spheres of influence and areas of occupation. The Nazis breached the pact by launching a major offensive against the Soviet Union on June 22, 1941.

**Treblinka** A labour and death camp created as part of Operation Reinhard, the German code word for the Nazi plan to murder Jews in German-occupied Poland using poison gas. From July 1942 to October 1943 more than 750,000 Jews were killed at Treblinka, making it second to Auschwitz in the numbers of Jews killed in a Nazi camp. Treblinka was liberated by the Soviet army in July 1944.

**United Nations Relief and Rehabilitation Administration** (UNRRA) An international relief agency created at a 44-nation conference in Washington, DC, on November 9, 1943, to provide economic assistance and basic necessities to war refugees. It was especially active in repatriating and assisting refugees in the formerly Nazi-occupied European nations immediately after World War II.

**Uriel Acosta** (1590–1647) A Portuguese-born writer and philosopher who was excommunicated by the Amsterdam Jewish community. A Yiddish play based on his life was written by Karl Gutzkow in 1847.

*Volksdeutsche* The term used for ethnic Germans who lived outside Germany in Central and Eastern Europe; also refers to the ethnic German colonists who were resettled in Polish villages as part of far-reaching Nazi plans to Germanize Nazi-occupied territories in the East.

**Wannsee Conference** A meeting held in Berlin on January 20, 1942, where high-ranking Nazi Party members and members of the German government met to discuss the implementation of the "Final Solution to the Jewish Question" – the euphemistic term referring to the Nazis' plan to systematically murder Europe's Jewish population.

*yahrzeit* (Yiddish) The commemoration of the anniversary of a Jewish person's death by the child, spouse, sibling or parent of the deceased. It is observed on the anniversary of the relative's death according to the Jewish lunar calendar.

**yeshiva** (Hebrew) A Jewish educational institution in which religious texts such as the Torah and Talmud are studied.

**Yiddish** A language derived from Middle High German with elements of Hebrew, Aramaic, Romance and Slavic languages, and written in Hebrew characters. Spoken by Jews in east-central Europe for roughly a thousand years from the tenth century to the mid-twentieth century, it was still the most common language among European Jews until the outbreak of World War II. There are similarities between Yiddish and contemporary German.

**Zionist and Jewish movements in interwar Poland** Among the significant Jewish political movements that flourished in Poland before World War II were various Zionist parties – the General Zionists; the Labour Zionists (Poalei Zion); the Revisionist Zionists formed under Ze'ev Jabotinsky; and the Orthodox Religious Zionists (the Mizrachi movement) – and the entirely secular and socialist Jewish Workers' Alliance, known as the Bund. Although Zionism and Bundism were both Jewish national movements and served as Jewish political parties in interwar Poland, Zionism advocated a Jewish national homeland in the Land of Israel, while Bundism advocated Jewish cultural autonomy in the Diaspora. A significant number of Polish Jews in the interwar years preferred to affiliate with the non-Zionist religious Orthodox party, Agudath Israel. *See also* Agudath Israel; Mizrachi; and Poalei Zion.

Photographs

1

2

1 David's maternal grandfather, Eliezer Dajtelbaum. Chmielnik, date unknown.
2 David's grandmother, uncles and aunts. Chmielnik, date unknown.

1   Itchele Neiman, David's father. Chmielnik, circa 1930.

2   David, age 10, with sisters Tova Leah, age 12, and Faigele, age 4. Chmielnik, 1929.

David's future wife, Hanka (second from right, on bicycle), and Hanka's aunt Esther (third from left), en route to Lodz after liberation. 1945.

1 & 2  Nazi-issued documents – prisoner card and personal effects card –  relating to David Newman in Buchenwald. 1945.

Identity document certifying that David Newman (Najman) was held in Buchenwald during the war. Landsberg, 1946.

Anna Newman's identity document, 1946.

1 David and Hanka on their wedding day. Lodz, October 14, 1945.
2 Wedding photo with Hanka's aunt Esther. Lodz, October 14, 1945.
3 David and Hanka with their son, Isaac (Jack). Landsberg, December 1946.
4 Isaac, age 1. Paris, 1947.

1

2

1 David and Hanka (centre) with cousins and friends. Paris, 1947.
2 With family in Paris. In the back row: David's uncle Charles (left) and David. Front row (left to right): Isaac, Aunt Fela, Hanka and Toni, daughter of Uncle Charles and Aunt Fela. Paris, 1951.

Family portrait in Paris. Back row (left to right): David's cousin Arlette; Hanka; David; and David's cousin Fernand. Middle row (centre): Hanka's aunt Esther and her husband, Leon. In front: Isaac and cousin Sabina. Paris, circa 1949.

David Newman. Paris, circa 1950.

1  Isaac (Jack) and his cousin Sabina. Paris, summer 1950.
2  Hanka and Isaac (Jack) on the ship *General Taylor*, headed for Halifax. April 1951.

David (second from left) who was asked to be the cantor but decided instead to be in the choir at the Hebrew Men of England Synagogue. Toronto, 1951.

David and Hanka dancing at a gathering of Tarnów landsmen. Toronto, 1953.

1 & 2  David and Hanka with members of Club Ten, a group of Holocaust survivor couples who formed a surrogate extended family. Toronto, 1950s and 1960s.

1 & 2  David and Hanka with their Club Ten friends. Toronto, 1970s and 1980s.

1 David's daughter, Gloria, on her wedding day. Left to right: David, Hanka, Gloria and Jack. Toronto, 1970s.
2 David and his daughter, Gloria.

1 David (far left) in the advertisement for the theatrical production of *Come Blow Your Horn*.

2 David playing the role of the father in *Come Blow Your Horn*.

David meeting Israeli president Ephraim Katzir. Jerusalem, 1973.

3

1 David teaching Yiddish. Toronto, 1995.

2 David (centre) with students Rabbi Korn and Lou Gula. Toronto, 1995.

3 David (far right) with his students at the Adath Israel Congregation. Toronto, 1995.

# Index

The Azrieli Foundation was established in 1989 to realize and extend the philanthropic vision of David J. Azrieli, C.M., C.Q., M.Arch. The Foundation's mission is to support a wide spectrum of initiatives in education and research. The Azrieli Foundation is an active supporter of programs in the fields of Education, the education of architects, scientific and medical research, and the arts. The Azrieli Foundation's many initiatives include: the Holocaust Survivor Memoirs Program, which collects, preserves, publishes and distributes the written memoirs of survivors in Canada; the Azrieli Institute for Educational Empowerment, an innovative program successfully working to keep at-risk youth in school; the Azrieli Fellows Program, which promotes academic excellence and leadership on the graduate level at Israeli universities; the Azrieli Music Project, which celebrates and fosters the creation of high-quality new Jewish orchestral music; and the Azrieli Neurodevelopmental Research Program, which supports advanced research on neurodevelopmental disorders, particularly Fragile X and Autism Spectrum Disorders.